Cambridge Elements

Elements in Comparative Political Theory
edited by
Leigh K. Jenco
London School of Economics

THE PLURALISTIC FRAMEWORKS OF IBN RUSHD AND ABDULLAHI AHMED AN-NA'IM

Ayesha Omar
*University of the Witwatersrand
and SOAS, University of London*

CAMBRIDGE
UNIVERSITY PRESS

CAMBRIDGE
UNIVERSITY PRESS

Shaftesbury Road, Cambridge CB2 8EA, United Kingdom

One Liberty Plaza, 20th Floor, New York, NY 10006, USA

477 Williamstown Road, Port Melbourne, VIC 3207, Australia

314–321, 3rd Floor, Plot 3, Splendor Forum, Jasola District Centre, New Delhi – 110025, India

103 Penang Road, #05–06/07, Visioncrest Commercial, Singapore 238467

Cambridge University Press is part of Cambridge University Press & Assessment, a department of the University of Cambridge.

We share the University's mission to contribute to society through the pursuit of education, learning and research at the highest international levels of excellence.

www.cambridge.org
Information on this title: www.cambridge.org/9781009517300

DOI: 10.1017/9781009386333

© Ayesha Omar 2025

This publication is in copyright. Subject to statutory exception and to the provisions of relevant collective licensing agreements, no reproduction of any part may take place without the written permission of Cambridge University Press & Assessment.

When citing this work, please include a reference to the DOI 10.1017/9781009386333

First published 2025

A catalogue record for this publication is available from the British Library

ISBN 978-1-009-51730-0 Hardback
ISBN 978-1-009-38632-6 Paperback
ISSN 2633-3597 (online)
ISSN 2633-3589 (print)

Cambridge University Press & Assessment has no responsibility for the persistence or accuracy of URLs for external or third-party internet websites referred to in this publication and does not guarantee that any content on such websites is, or will remain, accurate or appropriate.

The Pluralistic Frameworks of Ibn Rushd and Abdullahi Ahmed An-Na'im

Elements in Comparative Political Theory

DOI: 10.1017/9781009386333
First published online: January 2025

Ayesha Omar
University of the Witwatersrand and SOAS, University of London

Author for correspondence: Ayesha Omar, ao32@soas.ac.uk

Abstract: The purpose of this Element is to analyse the assiduous attempts of two Islamic political thinkers – the twelfth-century Andalusian philosopher Ibn Rushd and the contemporary Sudanese reformist Abdullahi Ahmed An-Na'im – to theorise Islamic politics through what this Element calls 'pluralistic frameworks'. A pluralistic framework is a systematic mediation of Islamic ethics and politics that incorporates extra-Islamic traditions of thought from diverse sources. Pluralistic frameworks selectively and self-consciously enable dialogue, synthesis, and hybridity and seek to maintain a distinct conception of Islamic ethics that concords with a preferred set of political arguments. They enable reflexivity within the ethical purview of Islam and with an awareness of the normativity of *sharī'a*. Both Ibn Rushd and An-Na'im reconcile *sharī'a* in two very different ways, but to a common end; Ibn Rushd lays out a method of harmonisation with Greek thought, while An-Na'im resorts to the radical subversion of *sharī'a* under liberal thought.

Keywords: Ibn Rushd, An-Na'im, pluralistic frameworks, Islamic ethics, politics

© Ayesha Omar 2025

ISBNs: 9781009517300 (HB), 9781009386326 (PB), 9781009386333 (OC)
ISSNs: 2633-3597 (online), 2633-3589 (print)

Contents

1 Islamic Ethics and Politics   1

2 Harmonising Greek Thought and *Sharīʿa*:
The Pluralistic Framework of Ibn Rushd   20

3 Negotiating *Sharīʿa* and Liberal Thought: The Pluralistic
Framework of Abdullahi Ahmed An-Na'im   39

4 Rethinking Islamic Politics: Pluralistic Frameworks
and the Future   58

Bibliography   70

1 Islamic Ethics and Politics

The link between Islamic ethics and politics is an enduring theme in Islamic thought from the premodern era to the present day.[1] It features in a myriad of Islamic conceptual frameworks and theoretical imaginaries that seek to reimagine the link between Islamic ethics and politics in complex, enigmatic, and innovative ways. Such frameworks are not confined to traditional political treatises or handbooks of government. They are found in a range of legal, philosophical, and theological texts and sources discussing the relative status of reason and revelation, the centrality of Islamic positive law, and the role of legal methods in determining political and ethical action. Such frameworks are sometimes pluralistic in that they incorporate extra-Islamic traditions of political thought from a diverse range of sources. The inclusion of these extra-Islamic sources of thought demonstrates a particular kind of reflexivity that reimagines and reshapes the contours of Islamic political thought within a broadly Islamic ethical purview.[2] Islamic political thought is therefore as much an ethical tradition as it is a political tradition.

To better understand the Islamic ethical tradition, it is important to define what is meant by ethics and consider how it may differ from morality, as these conceptual categories are often treated interchangeably. In this Element, I understand ethics as the study of morality or moral questions which considers how beliefs (including those derived from religious doctrine and foundational texts) are formed by making moral judgements about right and wrong. As is the case with a religious tradition like Islam, moral content which shapes doctrine and belief is extracted from commandments and precepts of the Qur'an as a foundational text of scripture, and the *Sunnah*, the exemplification of these precepts in the Prophetic sayings and life conduct. Ethics in Islam can be understood in two broad senses. Since Islam offers a systematic normative standard for working out right and prescribed conduct through the methodology of law, ethics interacts with and is informed by law. Yet Islamic ethical theories are also presented through other methods including rationalising and philosophical approaches. This has widened the scope for articulating Islamic ethical and moral values outside of juristically defined methods (Nanji, 1991, p. 111). In this latter iteration, ethics can be thought of as the study of moral principles, values, and conduct principally through the foundational sources. Taken together, both these senses of understanding ethics capture how Islamic ethics is derived from revealed sources but also develops its own modes of

---

[1] By Islam/ic I refer to *Sunnism*, the dominant branch of Islam in the Muslim world.
[2] The term *extra-Islamic* is useful because it recognises the distinctiveness of something outside a category while simultaneously allowing for the possibility of its inclusion.

inquiry. It is both grounded in scriptural morality and open to (and limited by) wider philosophical exploration.

The purpose of this Element is to analyse the comprehensive and systematic attempts of two Islamic political thinkers – the twelfth-century Andalusian philosopher Ibn Rushd and the contemporary Sudanese reformist Abdullahi Ahmed An-Na'im – to theorise Islamic politics through this approach, which I refer to as a 'pluralistic framework'. A pluralistic framework can be defined as a systematic mediation of Islamic ethics and politics that incorporates extra-Islamic traditions of political thought from a diverse range of sources. Pluralistic frameworks selectively and self-consciously enable dialogue, synthesis, and hybridity with extra-Islamic sources while maintaining a distinct conception of Islamic ethics that concords with a preferred set of political arguments but with an awareness of the normativity of *sharī'a*. As I outline in the forthcoming section, Ibn Rushd and An-Na'im negotiate *sharī'a* in two very different ways, but to a common end. Ibn Rushd lays out a method of harmonisation with Greek thought, while An-Na'im resorts to *sharī'a*'s radical subversion under the instruments of liberal political thought. The common refrain of their pluralistic frameworks is that they advocate ambiguity, flexibility, and theological innovation, which departs from the 'methods and sensibilities' of the Islamic tradition. Since *sharī'a* functions as indispensable to Muslim self-identification and self-understanding, such departures may undermine the principle of plausibility in the mediation of Islamic ethics and politics.

The concept of *sharī'a* is fundamental to how Muslims perceive and define themselves as 'inheritors of an objective, ascertainable and realisable divine truth' (Abou El Fadl, 2013, p. 10). It represents an authoritative system of normative beliefs and practices inscribed by an ethical fervour. As Hallaq argues: '[t]o be a Muslim individual today is to be, in fundamental ways, connected with that *sharī'a*-defined ethic, for it is this ethic that shaped what Islam is and has been . . . There is no Muslim identity without this ethic' (Hallaq, 2013, p. 70). Among believing Muslims, *sharī'a* thus holds the strongest claim to express what is considered normative and prescribed conduct for a meaningful ethical life.[3] *Sharī'a* encompasses a wide range of sources that defer to human reason. While the Qur'an is the primary source and foundational text, it is supplemented by the *Sunnah* (the life and traditions of the Prophet Muhammad), *qiyās* (analogical or deductive reasoning), and *ijmā'* (the consensus of Muslim jurists). This normative system, formalised through the science and methods of Islamic jurisprudence (*usūl al-fiqh*) in the eighth century, came to be termed *sharī'a*. While the Qur'an and Hadith remain the central texts for

---

[3] This is true despite the varying levels to which *sharī'a* might be practically observed.

extrapolating legal rulings, *sharī'a*, as a normative system of law, is dynamic and applied. Its evolution is contingent on the application of human reason which is enacted through the traditional use of consensus in sustaining legal normativity. The field of Islamic jurisprudence ensures that Islamic ethics are derived from and intertwined with moral law.

The absence of a clear division between ethics and politics in Islam is a consequence of *sharī'a* offering a set of moral guidelines for socio-ethical living. Few would dispute that the book of revelation – the Qur'an – is revered by Muslims as a divine and authoritative source of morality. The Qur'an is both the source of morality *and* the foundation from which broader principles of virtuous social and political living can be extrapolated. March describes this 'theocentricity' of ethical values, norms, and commands as Islam's normative revolution from Arabian paganism: 'God Himself is referred to in ethical terms (many of the Names of God refer to ethically salient features of God's essential nature) and man's attitude towards God is the primary criterion of moral evaluation' (March, 2012, p. 204). Yet, to be clear, the Qur'an does not offer a comprehensive and definitive set of political guidelines or a political theory. Neither does it contain directives on the origin, nature, and limits of political authority nor on the form of governance or institutions that constitute an ideal state. Instead, the Qur'an articulates themes, concepts, and ideas related to ethical life (Tampio, 2014, p. 2). This includes the importance of establishing a just and moral community. The gap between moral law and positive political arrangements is left to Islamic positive law to bridge, by articulating in more detail the norms and values required for public life. Such an articulation depends on the instrumentalities of human reason.

The Qur'an does not also contain an ethical theory in the strict sense but 'embodies the whole of the Islamic ethos' (Fakhry, 1991, p. 1). Its ethical teachings are woven through its verses, which contain parables, narratives, and poetical imagery. Qur'anic ethics interspersed through Qur'anic verses captures the 'spirit of (*hilm*) clemency, kindness (*ihsan*) in human relations, justice ('*adl*), avoiding what is wrong (*zulm*), abstinence, control of passions, and the rejection of pride and arrogance' (Leaman, 2014, p. 110). These ethical principles are inferred as constituting the basis for virtuous social and political living. The Qur'an does not therefore systematise ethics into a rigid theoretical or philosophical construct. However, in its scriptural entirety, it imparts ethical guidelines, moral lessons, and codes of conduct governing aspects of social and political life. As such, the search for a modern Islamic ethical theory, whether constituted through hermeneutical exegesis (*tafsir*) or some other method, leads back to the Qur'anic text as the primary source. The Qur'an and the *Sunnah* together embody the core of the Islamic ethical spirit. This is a distinguishing feature of the Islamic tradition.

The intersection of ethics and politics exists across numerous philosophical and religious traditions to varying degrees. What may distinguish Islam from these traditions more prominently is Islam's legalistic fusion with ethics and politics, a point that is usefully illustrated when analysing Islamic political history. In many premodern Islamic societies, the legislation of ethical conduct through *sharī'a* meant that Islam expanded its moral scope beyond individual virtue to the collective arena of social, legal, and political affairs. Ethical injunctions were often treated as legal imperatives that were administered by political officials and religious scholars (*ulama*) as a way of upholding virtue and justice for the entire political community of believers. Islamic intellectual history is richly laden with political treatises that explore the contours of this political arrangement.[4]

Conceptualising 'Pluralistic Frameworks'

Islamic thinkers have mediated the link between Islamic ethics and politics in innovative, creative, and complex ways. Two such attempts to reconcile *sharī'a* with the extra-Islamic traditions of Greek philosophy and liberal political thought can be observed in what I term the pluralistic frameworks of Ibn Rushd and Abdullahi Ahmed An-Na'im. As defined earlier in this section, pluralistic frameworks constitute a systematic mediation of Islamic ethics and politics that incorporates extra-Islamic traditions of thought from a diverse range of sources. Pluralistic frameworks, I argue, actively seek to incorporate novel insights from extra-Islamic sources, including theories and philosophies that may, from the Islamic thinker's perspective, contain elements of truth or have demonstrated veracity through empirical validation. By harmonising these external truths with Islamic thought, pluralistic frameworks posit that alternative interpretations of *sharī'a* can be developed that concord with the ethical foundations of the Islamic tradition. Although pluralistic frameworks may not always be theorised or defended in explicitly Islamic terms, their distinguishing characteristic is to present claims within a broadly Islamic ethical purview. This dynamic interaction with a wide array of political concepts and ideas is for the purpose of theoretical argument. Pluralistic frameworks include acts of selective borrowing, dialogue, and hybridity that are often tactical and strategic. They

---

[4] These texts were concerned with defining what an ideal form of Islamic government or political authority may look like. See, for example, *Al-Ahkam al-Sultaniyyah* (*The Laws of Islamic Governance*) by Al-Mawardi (972–1058 CE). This influential work discusses the principles of Islamic government, the qualifications and duties of the *caliph* (ruler), and the administration of justice and public order in an Islamic polity.

frequently involve synthesising, elaborating, and revising ideas from a diverse array of extra-Islamic traditions of thought to advance new political arguments or to make normative recommendations for Islamic political reform. Pluralistic frameworks contain legal, philosophical, and sociological dimensions and are informed by changing political and social contexts. Fundamentally, they seek to broaden the scope of normative political inquiry by making new claims on the role of *sharī'a* in relation to politics and the state.

Pluralistic frameworks therefore operate at the level of epistemic and theoretical inquiry. Such inquiries are expansive and creative, displaying a willingness to incorporate and adapt extra-Islamic political concepts and ideas and employing them in specific contexts. The most striking feature of such an approach is its methodological commitment to plurality itself. Pluralistic frameworks exhibit two broad elements of similarity at the level of theoretical inquiry. The first element is *epistemological flexibility*. This is characterised by the recognition and accommodation of multiple 'valid' ways of acquiring and validating knowledge within the Islamic intellectual tradition. Epistemological flexibility is marked by the desire to establish intersections and commonalities between disparate sources to advance new approaches in Islamic thinking, whether radical, agnostic, or unorthodox. The idea of flexibility demonstrates an intellectual openness to consider various interpretations, perspectives, and sources of knowledge and to counterbalance the promising insights of these claims in light of an already established conception of Islamic normativity. Epistemological flexibility fosters a more inclusive and adaptable approach to political questions.

Epistemological flexibility is followed by a second related element, namely *comfort with ambiguity*. Comfort with ambiguity refers to the willingness to accept and engage with the inherent complexities, uncertainties, and lack of definitive answers that often arise in the realm of normative theory. Such a willingness embraces ambiguity and transcends the constraints of any single mode of reasoning or finite human world view. Ambiguity in the context of a pluralistic framework is not viewed as antithetical to Islam but as crucial to the project of harmonising reason and revelation. As Baueur (2021) suggests, Islamic intellectual history reflects a conflict between two distinct orientations: one seeks to eliminate all uncertainties and to establish undisputed, ultimate truths, while the other, in contrast, contends with ambiguity and embraces complexity. This notion of a 'tolerance of ambiguity', as Bauer terms it, is evident in Islamic texts of law, politics, hermeneutics, and literature (Bauer, 2021, p. 1). Pluralistic frameworks are useful in providing content and meaning to Bauer's conception of the culture of ambiguity. Foregrounding the ambiguity, equivocality, and complexity of Islamic political thought emphasises the contrast with the orientalist notion of its narrowness and absolutism.

In discussing the pluralistic frameworks of these two Islamic thinkers, I adopt an analytical approach that largely (but not entirely) avoids normative interjections. Instead, I focus on identifying the recurring patterns in their political questioning and on how their arguments relate to their mediation of Islamic ethics and politics. It is true that the particular and subtle techniques utilised by these thinkers to achieve this goal are not fully aligned, nor are their claims, purposes, or projects similar. To suggest this would be somewhat contrived and historically anachronistic. Like all thinkers in the history of political thought, Ibn Rushd and An-Na'im are products of their time and context. Moreover, they are Islamic thinkers from two distinct historical eras separated by some *eight centuries*. This temporal distance does not preclude the possibility of meaningful comparative inquiry so often sequestered by the question of modernity and born from the tendency to treat different historical periods as entirely separate and disconnected through a contrived historical chasm.[5] Rather than get mired in debates around modernity, this Element questions the primacy accorded to historicist frameworks which impose a false theoretical and methodological dominance by questioning the hegemony of history.[6]

Yet admittedly the comparative nature of this inquiry is complicated by tremendous historical variance. The historical context of twelfth-century Muslim Spain was defined by the shifting political exigencies of Almohad imperial rule. This is reflected in Ibn Rushd's personal biography, where his roles as a philosopher, court physician (*ṭabīb*), and grand judge (*qāḍī*) were facilitated by a peculiar form of court patronage. Likewise, the institutional arrangements of Almohad society were marked by medieval and premodern imperatives, principally the role of the imperial ruler (*caliph*), religious courts administered in line with Maliki law, and the influence of religious scholars (*ulamā*) on the political community. While Ibn Rushd's philosophic endeavours were enabled by the rationalising spirit of the Almohad caliphate, his engagement with extra-Islamic traditions of Greek thought forms part of a *longue durée* of philosophical engagement by Islamic thinkers like Al-Farabi and Ibn Sina over the preceding two centuries. Notably, while Greek thought formed the foundation of the European intellectual canon, it held an equally seminal position within the Islamic philosophical tradition of that era. Ibn Rushd took this project further by developing a sophisticated methodological statement in

---

[5] Here I am suggesting that comparative inquiries between thinkers across different eras are often isolated, confined, or marginalised due to preoccupations or concerns regarding the concept of modernity (i.e. the modern age, modern thought, etc.).

[6] The concepts of a *hegemony of history* and the critique of hegemonic historical narratives have been further developed and expanded upon by other postcolonial theorists, such as Gayatri Spivak, Homi K. Bhabha, and Dipesh Chakrabarty, as well as scholars in the field of subaltern studies and critical historiography.

favour of the harmonisation between Islamic thought and Greek philosophical precepts. This contribution alone makes him an exemplar thinker within the Islamic tradition and the progenitor, if we like, of the importance of the pluralistic method. It is a telling fact about the innovative nature of his approach that this contribution is better recognised today than in his own time. Ostensibly, as a legal scholar, he conforms in more rigid ways to the bounds of Islamic normativity, but this stands in contrast to his political commentaries and philosophical treatises where he seeks to harmonise *sharī'a* with Greek philosophy by ascribing a tremendous role to human reason. In Section 2, I provide an account of his pluralistic framework and show how it is grounded in his novel theory of Islamic ethics, which is a systematic attempt to unify *sharī'a* with Aristotelian philosophy and to harmonise reason with revelation.

An-Na'im is a Sudanese American legal scholar and professor of law. The central features of his biography include his early education, legal training, experiences of civil war, imprisonment, and political exile.[7] These latter aspects directly inform the tenor of his political thought, which promotes a radical, Islamic legal and political reform. Of singular importance is the impact of the Second Sudanese Civil War, a twenty-year conflict that fractured Sudanese society for decades to come. For An-Na'im, the deleterious impact of the civil war can be traced to a policy shift in 1983 by President Ja'far Nimeiry in a political move which converted Sudan into an Islamic state under *sharī'a* law. Islamist factions like the National Islamic Front were co-opted to introduce harsh penal codes and restrictions on personal freedoms, leading to wide-scale persecution, including that of the Christian population in the south. An-Na'im's reflections on these events have profoundly shaped his assessment of Islam in the postcolonial world. Writing for a contemporary Muslim audience, he grapples with the challenges Islamic postcolonial societies are confronted with amid global capitalism, nation state formation, and technological change. Critically, he seeks a solution negotiating *sharī'a* within a liberal world order. Inspired by his spiritual and intellectual mentor, Mahmoud Mohamed Taha, An-Na'im is committed to reconciling Islamic values with those of liberal modernity. He views the damage colonialism has inflicted on the political and ethical structures of Muslim social life as a pernicious yet pragmatic reality. Consequently, he suggests that Islamic ethics must be radically reformed by appealing to a hermeneutic method that departs from Islamic tradition. As I explore in Section 3, in his pluralistic framework, such a method aligns with his liberal orientation, which seeks to incorporate aspects of the Rawlsian liberal tradition

---

[7] The biographical aspects of An-Na'im's life are extracted from an interview I conducted with Professor Abdullahi An-Na'im at the Centre for Law and Religion at the University of Emory (15 April 2023).

to advance a theory of a secular state in Islam where *sharī'a* is negotiated through a kind of overlapping consensus. While An-Na'im's political thought can be situated within a longer tradition of engagement by Islamic reformist thinkers with liberal ideas, I explore how a liberal, human rights discourse remains at the centre of his approach.[8]

Despite the variances of historical context I have already noted, my argument is to suggest that both Ibn Rushd and An-Na'im adopt pluralistic frameworks which enable a peculiar form of methodological and conceptual reflexivity in their mediation of Islamic ethics and politics. These pluralistic frameworks selectively and self-consciously enable dialogue, synthesisation, and hybridity with the extra-Islamic traditions of Greek philosophy and liberal political thought while advancing a distinct conception of Islamic ethics that concords with their preferred set of political arguments. Within a broadly Islamic ethical purview, I suggest that both these thinkers reconcile the normativity of *sharī'a* in innovative and unorthodox ways, but with a common end; Ibn Rushd lays out a method of harmonisation with Greek thought, while An-Na'im resorts to the radical subversion of *sharī'a* under the instruments of liberal political thought. As we shall see more fully in Sections 2 and 3, the fact that these thinkers self-consciously aim to influence a Muslim audience serves to highlight a set of common challenges for mediating ethics and politics in Islam. In my analysis of these challenges, I seek to also bring to the fore the difficulty of theorising the notion of an Islamic orthodoxy, a term that is both elusive and muddied insofar as it denotes distinct, overlapping, and even contradictory meanings in Islamic scholarship.[9]

Pluralistic Frameworks: The Challenges of Mediating Islamic Ethics and Politics

Navigating the complex terrain of Islamic law and ethics discloses several key challenges for Islamic thinkers concerned with theorising politics through pluralistic frameworks. Such challenges often relate to enduring debates that manifest in Islamic political thought across space and time on the place of reason, revelation, authority, and methodology. Outlining the contours of these challenges is useful insofar as they relate to broader questions of the Islamic tradition, its perceived singularity, or what constitutes its essence.[10] Asad's formulation of

---

[8] The engagement of Islamic thinkers with liberal thought reflects a complex dialogue between tradition and modernity, religion and secularism, and local values and global ideologies. This ongoing conversation shapes the intellectual landscape of contemporary Islamic political thought. Scholars such as Hourani (1983), March (2011), and Iqtidar (2017) instantiate the complex contours of this engagement.

[9] On the nomenclature of Islamic orthodoxy, see Wilson (2008).

[10] On orthodoxy and essentialist and anti-essentialist approaches in the study of Islam, see Sulaiman (2018).

The Pluralistic Frameworks   9

Islam as a 'discursive tradition' is especially pertinent for answering these questions and for thinking about Islam beyond reductive and essentialising tropes (Asad, 2009). Central to Asad's argument is to consider Islam as a tradition of Muslim discourse with its own past: 'the important point about tradition ... is simply that all instituted practices are oriented to a conception of the past' (Asad, 2009, p. 21). For Asad, the Islamic tradition 'includes and relates itself to the founding texts of the Qur'an and the Hadith' and the discursive relationship of Muslims with these texts is paramount in its articulation (Asad, 1986, p. 14). What Asad provides us is a valuable starting point or 'bedrock' from which the term *Islam* can be constituted. In other words, Islam is moored to foundational texts which embed its tradition in a universe of meaning (Wilson, 2008, p. 182). As Anjum notes, 'Muslims all agree – to the extent that an agreement is possible in a complex world tradition – to begin somewhere ... [Islam] is a relationship with certain foundational texts and a particular historical narrative of their origins' (Anjum, 2007, p. 667).[11] For Anjum, Asad's recognition of foundational texts as central to the Islamic discursive tradition is akin to a universal orthodoxy in Islam, distinct from shifting forms of local orthodoxy (Anjum, 2007, p. 667). In other words, a universal orthodoxy in Islam always designates a range of acceptable beliefs and practices (Wilson, 2008, p. 144). This distinction, I argue, allows us to traverse the knotty conceptual language of Islamic orthodoxy more easily. Its valence is illuminated in the three challenges for mediating Islamic ethics and politics that I present next.

The first challenge concerns ethics. In my analysis, I underscore how both Ibn Rushd and An-Na'im confront (whether explicitly or implicitly) a key theological conundrum on the limits of reason and the place of rationalism in Islam. Medieval Islamic theological debates were fixated on resolving this conundrum by positing various theories regarding whether God's commands are beyond human approval, rejection, or alteration.[12] Vast tracts of writing emanating from early Islamic thought, for example, were dedicated to the theological question of whether morality is subjectively willed by God as opposed to existing objectively and

---

[11] Anjum (2007) develops Asad's conception of an Islamic discursive tradition and its relationship to the question of orthodoxy more concretely. He introduces the distinction between orthodoxy-as-power (local orthodoxy) and Orthodoxy (universal religious orthodoxy) to elucidate the complex nature of orthodoxy in Islam. Anjum underscores the interpretive nature of Muslim engagement with foundational texts, emphasising that universal orthodoxy allows for varied local articulations rather than imposing a singular interpretation. Additionally, Anjum explores the coexistence of multiple local orthodoxies within Islam, highlighting the dynamic and evolving nature of orthodoxy influenced by socio-historical contexts and discursive traditions (Anjum, 2007, p. 667). This distinction is useful for this Element, which seeks to eschew reductive and essentialised readings of Islamic concepts.

[12] For more on traditionalism and rationalism in classical Islamic theological debates, see Makdisi (1991).

independently of God's freely willed choice. But these debates were hardly settled and continued to elicit a variety of perspectives of Islamic rationalism. Intellectual historians of Islam also remain divided on whether 'theistic subjectivism' emerges as the dominant moral theology of Islam, in which God, not human beings, is proclaimed the decider of values (Makdisi, 1991; Hourani, 1985; Jackson, 2009).[13] For example, Jackson disputes Hourani's early formulation of 'theistic subjectivism' or the notion that value, particularly concepts of good and evil as solely determined by external sources such as scripture or divine decrees, can be deemed an orthodox Islamic position. Jackson presents an alternative perspective that emphasises the role of human reasoning, interpretation, and ethical deliberation in shaping moral values within Islamic theological discourse as a more dominant approach (Jackson, 2009, pp. 83–87). Considering these dynamics within Islamic ethical debates is important for understanding the fluidity of authoritative religious discourse at different moments in Islamic history which were invariably influenced by power. It further suggests that the nomenclature of an Islamic orthodoxy can be elusive in evaluating the history of political thought.

The second challenge relates to the centrality of *sharī'a* in shifting historical contexts. Claiming *sharī'a*'s link to a universal Islamic orthodoxy, I suggest, is a somewhat easier task if we acknowledge *sharī'a* as an instantiation of the universal orthodoxy of foundational texts in Islam's discursive tradition.[14] The challenge for both Ibn Rushd and An-Na'im centres on responding to the normative centrality of *sharī'a* as a formalised and accepted tradition of legal jurisprudence and as a set of norms with a teleological end, the well-being and welfare of the political community. This latter conception holds the purpose of *sharī'a* as the means to the way of God and the pathway of goodness and virtue; its objective is not simply compliance with

---

[13] On the question of Islamic ethics, some Islamic intellectual historians such as Sherman Jackson argue that theistic subjectivism does not constitute the Islamic orthodoxy, in that it was a relatively late development, and three of the four Muslim theological schools (Atharis, Maturidis, and Mu'tazila – the first two would be considered Sunni, while the last came to dominate among the Shi'a) adopt some version of rational ethical objectivism, making A'sharite subjectivism a minority (Jackson, 2009).

[14] Anjum's main argument revolves around the significance of universal orthodoxy in Islamic discursive tradition, with *sharī'a* serving as a key component that contributes to the formation and expression of such a universal orthodoxy. Anjum contends that universal orthodoxy serves as a limit that preserves Islam's singularity (Anjum, 2007, p. 667). As such, my use of the term *orthodoxy* in relation to these thinkers applies to the tradition of Islamic legal theory where a canonisation process facilitated by the production and circulation of key texts, and supported by scholarly networks, educational institutions (*madrasas*), and political patronage reified authoritative discourse (El Shamsy, 2013, pp. 117–120). This canonisation had far-reaching implications for Islamic thought and practice, providing a shared methodology for deriving legal rulings and contributing to the perception of Islamic law as a unified and coherent system, while still allowing for ongoing debates and diverse perspectives within the canonical tradition. Crucially, it established an authoritative framework for Islamic jurisprudence.

the commands of God for their own sake. As Abou El Fadl points out, compliance is regarded as a means to an end – 'the serving of the physical and spiritual welfare and well-being of people' (Abou El Fadl, 2013, p. 11). Both Ibn Rushd and An-Na'im recognise the normative weight of *sharīʿa* in these two manifestations. For Ibn Rushd, the purpose of *sharīʿa* is to impart true knowledge of those actions by which the happiness of the whole of creation is guaranteed (Ibn Rushd, 1974, p. 316). Similarly, An-Na'im recognises that 'for Muslims *sharīʿa* is the *Whole Duty of Mankind*, moral and pastoral theology and ethics, high spiritual aspiration, and detailed ritualistic and formal observance; it encompasses all aspects of public and private good manners' (An-Na'im, 1990, p.11).

The third challenge centres on the degree to which incorporating extra-Islamic traditions of thought – whether Greek philosophy or liberal political thought – complicates the theoretical endeavour to mediate Islamic ethics and politics within the pluralistic framework. In other words, since *sharīʿa*, which includes a combination of textual hermeneutics and embodied practices, directly informs Islamic ethics, any pluralistic framework (that remains Islamic) must consequently account for the place of certain fundamental *sharīʿa* norms in politics. It is true that the choice of extra-Islamic sources utilised in a pluralistic framework will determine the degree of adaptation and reformulation required for preserving the link between Islamic ethics and politics and the extent to which a reconciliation with *sharīʿa* must take place. While both thinkers, I suggest, are concerned with preserving this link, their reconciliation of *sharīʿa* within the pluralistic framework is fundamentally different. Ibn Rushd, for example, finds tremendous congruence with Greek virtue ethics and *sharīʿa* and attempts to achieve harmonisation on this basis. An-Na'im distils from Rawlsian liberal political thought its most promising ideals, which he amends and reformulates to fit into a framework that subverts *sharīʿa* to liberal instruments. As such, I argue that the extent to which the mediation of Islamic ethics and politics may or may not appear convincing and compelling to its intended audience will likely depend on the basic underlying premise of the moral philosophy being utilised and its overall ability to reconcile with *sharīʿa*. In the case of these thinkers, I explore the limitations of their approaches in Section 4.

Are Pluralistic Frameworks Rare?

Borrowing concepts, synthesising ideas, and engaging in dialogue through the incorporation of extra-Islamic traditions of thought are familiar practices in Islamic intellectual history. The thinkers explored in this Element are therefore not isolated examples but are part of a continuum in the history of Islamic political thought. What then are the specific reasons for singling out these two figures as part of a comparative study of pluralistic frameworks? This question, I suggest, can be answered in two ways. First, on multiple readings of the political ideas of both thinkers, it became evident to me that An-Na'im draws upon Ibn Rushd explicitly for the purpose of positioning him as an exemplary thinker who venerates reason, plurality, and theological innovation within the Islamic tradition. In the process, the longevity of the pluralistic framework in Islamic thought became strikingly evident insofar as it related to three interrelated themes: the primacy of reason, the accommodation of diverse sources, and the openness to reinterpretation and reform. This pairing is therefore not a coincidental or arbitrary choice but a deliberate one, driven by a recognition of the resonances between their respective intellectual projects which engage with plurality in a systematic and comprehensive way.

Second, a common thread in the pluralistic approaches of both An-Na'im and Ibn Rushd is their unconventional reconciliation of *sharī'a* which departs from the traditional methods and sensibilities within the Islamic tradition. Such departures, I suggest, can be termed as unorthodox not for their mediation of Islamic ethics and politics or their incorporation of extra-Islamic traditions of thought but for their specific methods of harmonisation and subversion in reconciling *sharī'a* in a pluralistic framework. In the case of Ibn Rushd, this unorthodoxy manifests in his attempt to fit Islamic legal norms within the interstices of Greek philosophical thought. An-Na'im's unorthodoxy is reflected in his polemical theory of Islamic legal reform, which advocates for a radical reinterpretation of *sharī'a* to align with a modern liberal, human-rights-centred discourse. Arguably, the limitation of both these approaches lies in their departure from the established contours of the Islamic tradition to achieve alignment with a preferred set of normative political arguments (something I explore in Section 4). However, I am not proposing that such limitations render pluralistic frameworks unworkable endeavours for Islamic political theorisation in general. In fact, I am arguing quite the opposite. As I outline in Section 4, pluralistic frameworks can provide a useful structure for proposing new normative possibilities in modern Islamic political theory that can potentially circumvent such limitations. Such a circumvention hinges on the principle of remaining credible and authoritative to Muslim sensibilities.

Mediating Islamic Ethics and Politics in the Postcolonial

Pluralistic frameworks also tell us about the possibilities and limitations of mediating Islamic ethics and politics in the context of the unprecedented transformation of modern Islamic societies. This transformation, triggered by the colonial encounter and the subsequent formation of postcolonial Islamic nation states, profoundly disrupted the traditional socio-economic and political structures of Islamic societies. It introduced secularism, economic dependency, legal reform, cultural hegemony, and social change that created lasting tensions and disjuncture in the Muslim world. But perhaps its greatest encroachment was redefining the role of religion through a universalising logic of secularism through the institution of the modern sovereign state. For Hallaq, modern Muslims were faced with the challenge of reconciling two facts: 'first, the ontological fact of the state and its undeniably powerful presence, and second, the deontological fact of the necessity to bring about a form of *sharī'a* as governance' under this institutional form (Hallaq, 2013, p. 7). Hallaq argues that an *Islamic state* is both practically impossible and a theoretical contradiction in terms because colonialism not only eviscerated the existing systems of Islamic governance but also installed the institutional form of the modern sovereign state, which is sustained by moral objectives antithetical to *sharī'a*. Moreover, the modern sovereign state disassembled, codified, and redefined limited provisions of *sharī'a* for its political expediency and legitimacy, resulting in fragmentation and disjuncture (Hallaq, 2013, p. 18). Hallaq's critique of the modern state presents an exciting challenge for reimagining an institutional form of politics that transcends the sovereign state model and coheres better with the notion of Islamic ethics. Postcolonial Muslim states inscribed by colonial boundaries remain mired in religious sectarianism, social unrest, and political instability. The utility of this rethinking should therefore not be understated.

In response to Islam's encounter with modernity and colonialism, modern Islamic political thinkers have defended various positions in a contested attempt to reconcile Islamic ethics and politics. Islamic revivalist approaches encompass a diverse range of perspectives, from the theory of divine sovereignty as a counterweight to secular popular sovereignty, to more nuanced interpretations that emphasise the revival of Islamic principles and values within modern contexts. Curiously, the revivalist impulse, while often portrayed as a reactionary or oppositional force, contained normative dimensions that have deeply impacted the popular imagination of many Muslim-majority countries (Iqtidar & Scharbordt, 2022, p. 278). Its most ardent advocates, Maududi (1960) and Qutb (2006), for example, used the theory of divine sovereignty to posit the centrality of religion in all aspects of Muslim life. As a countenance to modernity, their ethico-political vision endeavoured to offer authentic Islamic solutions to modern social ills. Recent innovative readings of these influential thinkers offer alternative ways to understand their ideas and engagement with modernity (Euben, 1997; March, 2019; Iqtidar, 2021). These readings suggest that Islamic revivalist thinkers should be understood as part of a broader critique of rationalism and modernity, rather than mere reactionary responses. Maududi's Islamist thought, for example, creatively and reflexively engaged with various intellectual resources, combining elements from different traditions to reconcile the sovereignty of God with the sovereignty of the modern state (Iqtidar, 2020, p. 287). While Maududi's theo-democratic project ultimately reified rather than transcended the liberal, colonial state, revealing the limitations of mediating *sharī'a* with the sovereignty of the modern state (Iqtidar, 2020, p. 616), his theoretical accounts highlight the polyvalent forms of pluralistic engagement that are present within Islamist writing, and that are generally overlooked.

Similarly, Islamic 'democratic theorists' and 'modernists' have engaged in mediating between Islamic ethics and politics through varied liberalising approaches that pronounce Islam's compatibility with democracy, modern science, rationality, and legal reform. Prominent figures within this strand of thought, such as Fazlur Rahman (1982), Mohammed Arkoun (1994), and Abdolkarim Soroush (1998), have offered diverse perspectives on reinterpreting Islamic traditions and reconciling them with modern democratic principles and human rights frameworks. Their approaches range from advocating for a secular state with a separation of religion and politics to proposing reforms within the Islamic legal and political systems to align them with contemporary values and realities. There are of course historical reasons for the proliferation of these liberalising approaches in the postcolonial Islamic world. By the nineteenth century, liberalism, however multifariously defined, was imported into Muslim societies through colonialism. Colonised Muslim intellectuals were compelled to think about liberal values 'in cultural or religious terms' (Devji & Kazmi, 2017, p. 5). Moreover, by the end of the Cold War, postcolonial Islamic states found themselves firmly situated within a prevailing global liberal order.

By the late twentieth century, political theory was also dominated by a liberalism that was formulated through a rationalist epistemology and committed to reading the political world as 'knowable by way of human reason and methods' (Euben, 1999, p. 6). The paradox of the liberal theoretical endeavour to construct modern political society by rejecting the place of metaphysics, Euben argues, is that it occurred alongside a prevailing political reality that was quite the opposite (Euben, 1997, p. 28). Such a political reality included the Islamist turn towards foundationalism, which began to play a more prominent role in the global order. This Islamist turn towards foundationalism emphasised the centrality of divine revelation as the ultimate source of knowledge and for deriving Islamic ethical principles to guide all aspects of Muslim life, including politics and governance. This tension between the liberal theoretical endeavour and the Islamist foundationalist turn underscored the complexity of mediating Islamic ethics and politics within the modern context of postcolonial states.

How, then, can pluralistic frameworks offer normative possibilities that go beyond the Islamic foundationalist impulse and the liberal, post-foundationalist theoretical discourse? This is a challenge that An-Na'im must confront in his engagement with Rawls. Such an account must clarify how a comprehensive moral doctrine such as Islam can be reconciled with or adapted to a Rawlsian account of political liberalism. The extent to which Islam can be reconciled with moral pluralism while taking seriously the authority of Islamic legal normativity, or *sharī'a*, is at the heart of this analysis. As March contends, it is an inquiry that would involve a serious intellectual reckoning with 'what ought to be the balance between the desire to bring people to one's conception of truth' and the recognition of a reasonable moral pluralism in a diverse society (March, 2011, p. 182). Whether An-Na'im's pluralistic framework succeeds in answering these questions is something I consider in Section 3.

The Place of Ethics in Islamic and European Thought

Pluralistic frameworks in the modern context might also consider whether mediating Islamic ethics and politics requires dispensing with post-foundationalist, liberal imaginaries altogether. Here, the work of Alasdair MacIntyre is instructive.[15] For MacIntyre, it is the Enlightenment project, with its rational justification of individual autonomy and freedom, that fails to develop coherent moral teleology for modern life (MacIntyre, [1981] 2007, p. 51). In contrast to the Islamic tradition, where ethics and politics remained intrinsically linked, this connection was subject to major reconsideration in European philosophy from around the seventeenth century onwards. MacIntyre argues that the turn towards prioritising individual reason and rights represented a rupture with previous modes of moral theorising oriented towards higher goods and virtues. The reasons for this shift are complex and varied but include the rise of modern science, the scientific revolution, and the enhancement of rationalism. The social contract theories presented in Thomas Hobbes' *Leviathan* (1651) and John Locke's *Two Treatises on Government* (1689) are both attempts to separate politics and ethics at the level of abstract theoretical inquiry. Locke, for example, argued that political authority and jurisdiction originate in a social contract among equals. This contract is formed for the purpose of securing and protecting individual natural rights. For Locke, the role of the state

---

[15] In *After Virtue* ([1981] 2007), MacIntyre argues that moral pluralism is a result of the breakdown of traditional moral frameworks and the loss of a shared moral vocabulary. He contends that without such a shared vocabulary, moral disputes are ultimately irreconcilable. MacIntyre also critiques moral relativism, arguing that it similarly undermines the possibility of moral discourse and leads to a loss of moral principles. In *Whose Justice? Which Rationality?* (1988), MacIntyre engages with the work of other contemporary philosophers, including John Rawls, to provide a critique of moral pluralism.

was to ensure that these rights are protected; it is *not* to enforce a particular moral system or to legislate on ethical issues.

In general, modern Anglo-American political philosophy shifted away from the Aristotelian concern for moral virtue and towards the protection and recognition of individual rights and liberties. Aristotle's emphasis on constituting a societal order conducive to the highest virtues and conception of the good life was narrowed in scope to questions of negative liberties and rights. Politics was thus viewed as a domain concerned with the regulation of society and the distribution of power, and ethics was concerned with individual morality. Political philosophers such as Kant and John Stuart Mill still developed comprehensive moral philosophies, but these philosophies were defined in terms of universal duties, utility maximisation, or inviolable human rights rather than Aristotelian virtue. The shift from Aristotelian virtue ethics towards these deontological and consequentialist frameworks that emphasise individual rights, freedom, autonomy, and welfare represents a normative revolution in European philosophy. Kant's moral philosophy, for example, offered a deontological ethical framework based on the concept of duty and respect for individual moral autonomy (Kant, [1785] 2012) . In politics, this translated into an approach that prioritised individual rights and freedoms and the idea that the state should treat its citizens as autonomous moral agents. Following Kant, Rawls' political philosophy emphasised the capacity of individuals to engage in reasoning about principles of justice.

Kant's fundamental premises remain at odds with an Islamic ethical framework (however loosely defined), which highlights what is at stake in An-Na'im's project of mediating Islamic ethics and politics through the incorporation of liberal thought. That said, two general points require emphasis here. First, Kant operated within a secular framework separating moral principles from religious and theological foundations. His secular approach thus dismissed ethical claims rooted in religious or divine law when reimagining politics. Such secularism poses a profound challenge for Islamic political thinkers aiming to integrate Islamic values and principles into their political accounts.

Second, Kant places a strong emphasis on individual moral autonomy and the use of reason to determine moral duties. In contrast, Islamic political thought must confront the authority of Islamic legal normativity derived from sacred textual sources and traditions. While there is room for applying reason to ethical questions within the Islamic moral tradition, Islamic debates on the limits of human reason contrast sharply with Kant's emphasis on absolute rational autonomy. Reimagining Islamic ethics along Kantian lines of extreme individualism and rationalism could yield a more rights-based political approach, producing tensions between reason and revelation. The implications for politics depend on how this reconceptualised Islamic ethics engages with and is implemented within existing Islamic sociopolitical norms. Preserving core Islamic values remains crucial in the modern public and moral life of Muslim societies. Reconciling liberal thought with Islamic traditions thus requires carefully navigating this complex intersection between ethics and politics.

Harnessing the work of MacIntyre might be useful in this regard. The modern world's emphasis on individual choice and rights, rather than the moral judgement of a community, has weakened the authority of traditional moral frameworks while failing to provide a coherent and rational foundation for ethics, as MacIntyre claims. His premise is that different moral traditions contain incommensurable metaphysical elements, making it difficult to ground moral judgements in something more than subjective preference, ultimately undermining the idea of a common good (MacIntyre, 2007, p. 10). Seeking an alternative, MacIntyre advocates for the revival of virtue ethics, which understands moral action in relation to the purpose and good of a given community. This return to virtue ethics provides an ethical framework that offers a more robust and contextually grounded approach to morality. To develop this framework, MacIntyre draws on resources from the European tradition, including figures such as Plato, Aristotle, and Thomas Aquinas. As he rightly observes, rationality and ethics are embedded 'in a tradition, a conception according to which the standards of rational justification themselves emerge from and are part of a history in which they are vindicated' (MacIntyre, 1988, p. 7). Notably, Islam provides a formal foundational ethical system to define the notion of 'the good', which can be considered akin to the teleology of Greek virtue ethics (Kaminski, 2017, p. 22). MacIntyre's 'meta-theory of tradition-constituted enquiry' thus offers a way to balance the sanctity of scriptural sources, the relevance of intellectual traditions for interpretation, and the potential for reinterpretation in light of new experiences by engaging in empathetic dialogue with diverse traditions of thought (Harvey, 2023, p. 50). This approach provides a compelling theoretical foundation for Muslims to uphold their particular 'tradition-constituted' conceptions while also participating in pluralistic engagement with other traditions. Pluralistic frameworks exploring the mediation of Islamic ethics and politics could therefore find MacIntyre's work a valuable intellectual starting point. By employing McIntyre's arguments, Islamic pluralistic frameworks could seek to connect with these traditional sources of moral reasoning and practice and use them as a basis for constructive and collaborative engagement with contemporary ethical challenges. McIntyre's emphasis on shared moral vocabulary could also be useful in bridging the gap between traditional Islamic concepts and contemporary political discourse. As such, McIntyre's ideas might offer an alternative possibility, where the mediation of *sharī'a* presupposes a place for ethics by claiming the primacy of a tradition-constituted enquiry.

Transcending Binaries through Comparative Political Theory

Pluralistic frameworks can also serve to transcend the simplistic confines of the secular/Islamist binary, which presents an oversimplified categorisation of approaches to the role of Islam in politics. This binary reduces Islamic thought to two opposing poles: the 'secular', which advocates universalising the separation of religion from politics, and the 'Islamist', which assigns a central role to divine sovereignty in matters of governance. However, such a dichotomous framing ignores the rich subtleties and myriad forms of normative contestation that exist within the Islamic theoretical tradition itself. By casting Islam as caught between these two polarising positions, the secular/Islamist binary fails to capture the nuance, complexity, and diversity of thought and commitment within Islamic political theory. It disregards the plurality of perspectives, interpretations, and frameworks that have emerged from the Islamic tradition over centuries of scholarly engagement with questions of ethics, law, and politics. Foregrounding pluralistic frameworks presents an avenue to transcend this reductive binary approach. Such frameworks recognise and elucidate the dynamic interaction of Islamic ethics with both religious and philosophical currents across contexts. They underscore how Islamic thinkers have long grappled with mediating divine injunctions and ethical norms in conversation with other extra-Islamic traditions of moral and political thought.

My attempt to foreground pluralistic frameworks is not only intended as a repudiation of binary discourses that oversimplify and constrain the possibilities within Islamic political theory. Instead, it contributes to a richer understanding of the depth, heterogeneity, and polyvalent nature of Islamic intellectual history. Emphasising the subtleties of the Islamic tradition on its own terms, rather than through rigid conceptual binaries, I suggest, carries potentially emancipatory consequences for thinking about Islam and politics. First, it counters the tendency to view the Islamic tradition as inherently oppositional or alienating but as a discursive tradition ensconced in its own rich practices of conceptual and ethical meaning-making. A key illustration of this is the remarkable continuity within Islamic political thought around the centrality of *sharī'a* as a means of moral legitimation for governance. As An-Na'im observes, even practically, many contemporary Muslim-majority states continue to enlist the legitimising power of *sharī'a* in supporting a form of political authority (An-Na'im, 2008, p. 17).

Second, as Asad's (2003) path-breaking work reveals, there is no monolithic Islamic approach to ethics but rather a constant reconstruction and reinterpretation in response to changing social, historical, and political contexts. Aside from textual interpretations, Asad highlights how this process is shaped by evolving community practices, cultural norms, power relations, and social structures (Asad, 2003, p. 109).

The fact that Islamic thinkers across eras have grappled with mediating Islamic ethics and politics also reflects a particular form of intellectual dynamism that continues to endure. Recognising Islam's internal diversity and capacity for reimaging politics challenges narratives of irredeemable conflict with, for example, democratic norms. It also centres Muslims as rational agents continuously cocreating and negotiating ethical-political norms rather than as passive inheritors of monolithic doctrines.

Third, reading Islamic ethics and politics through the capacious lens of pluralistic frameworks speaks directly to the task of comparative political theory. As an 'immanent critique' (Jenco et al., 2020, p. 2), comparative theory identifies gaps and blind spots in mainstream political thought by drawing insights from traditions typically marginalised from its disciplinary core. Re-centring Islamic thinkers, texts, and ideas provides new substantive perspectives that can reshape and expand how we conceptualise political thought and ethics beyond the traditional European canon. This emancipates political theory from parochial limitations by pluralising its foundations. With its unique genealogies, methods frameworks, and interventions, Islamic political thought offers a revitalising counter discourse to the discipline's entrenched universalising tendencies frequently presented through European enlightenment liberalism. Edward Said's hugely influential text *Orientalism* (1978) makes a powerful case for why scholarship on Islam often constitutes misrepresentations founded on Eurocentric premises that serve imperial interests and power structures. Said's intervention offers conceptual and grammatical registers to identify, critique, and transcend the asymmetries and essentialism inherent in existing approaches to Islamic political theory.

One key task of comparative political theory, as articulated by Euben (1997), is to invoke comparison as a 'heuristic device' precisely to counter such biases – rendering Islamic ideas less unfamiliar and hostile by reading them on their own terms. This involves interrogating modes of analysis that are otherwise skewed or inadequate. For Euben, relinquishing prejudices and preconceptions about categories such as East/West or legitimate/illegitimate politics transforms how we relate to the unfamiliar (Euben, 1997, p. 8). I suggest pluralistic frameworks as a key idea that contributes in clarifying the distinctiveness of the Islamic tradition by illuminating how thinkers such as Ibn Rushd and An-Na'im reconcile *sharī'a* and mediate Islamic ethics and politics through dialogue, appropriation, and synthesisation with extra-Islamic traditions of thought. This approach acknowledges the deep intertwining of Islam with other intellectual traditions and underscores the complex historical interplay between Islamic and European ideas. It cautions against simplistic notions of 'cross-cultural dialogue', recognising that 'ideas travel and the politics of appropriation, reclamation, and misrecognition are central to the lives and afterlives of such ideas' (Jenco et al., 2020, p. 2).Fundamentally, it offers an analysis of Islamic political thought that recognises a foundational core which operates alongside diversity and pluralistic expression.

As a final point, then, I return to the question of comparison in relation to the thinkers I have chosen for this inquiry by addressing March's concern, which cautions against the temptation to single out 'unorthodox' Islamic figures such as Ibn Rushd and An-Na'im solely to challenge hostile caricatures of Islam (March, 2009, p. 556). March's insight prompts a crucial question: when we highlight these exemplary thinkers to illustrate the absence of profound conflict between civilisations or world views, how integral are they to the moral tradition under scrutiny? March urges rigorous consideration of whether we are genuinely engaging with the deep moral disagreements inherent in long-standing traditions when we focus on exemplar figures (March, 2009, p. 556). While these questions are significant, my inquiry seeks to do something quite different. In its critical examination of the pluralistic frameworks of Ibn Rushd and An-Na'im, this Element presents a genuinely reflective exercise in comparative political theory that emphasises the comprehensive and systematic mediation of Islamic ethics and politics by two remarkable thinkers across space and time. Rather than simply employing Ibn Rushd and An-Na'im as symbols to challenge misconceptions about Islam, it engages in a rigorous analysis that furnishes for illustration the complexities and inherent limitations of their attempts to develop pluralistic frameworks. There is tremendous critical purchase in a study that emphasises the latter point alone.

2 Harmonising Greek Thought and *Sharī'a*: The Pluralistic Framework of Ibn Rushd

The twelfth-century jurist and philosopher Abu'al-Walid Muhammad ibn Ahmad ibn Muhammad Ibn Rushd (1126–1198), known in Latin as Averroes, is widely regarded as one of the most extraordinary political thinkers and philosophers of the Islamic premodern tradition. Renowned for his role as a synthesiser of Aristotelian philosophy, his commentaries proved instrumental in the rediscovery of Greek philosophy in the Latin world. In this section, I examine how Ibn Rushd developed a pluralistic framework that mediated between Islamic ethics by harmonising *sharī'a* with the extra-Islamic tradition of Greek thought. Ibn Rushd's political thought, I suggest, was organised into two parts: an account of virtue ethics as prescribed by Aristotle in *Nicomachean Ethics* and a model of government and political authority as outlined by Plato in the *Republic*. While incorporating key elements from these extra-Islamic sources, I explore how Ibn Rushd advanced an original and sophisticated theory

The Pluralistic Frameworks 21

of politics that harmonised Platonic political concepts and ideas with Islam. This harmonisation, I contend, was undertaken within a pluralistic framework that combined the ethical precepts of *sharī'a* with Greek thought to mediate a distinct account of Islamic ethics and politics. My central claim is that Ibn Rushd's pluralistic approach was characterised by ambiguity, flexibility, and a distinctive theological innovation that posited a rationalistic Islamic ethics by declaring a harmonisation between Greek philosophy and *sharī'a* on the basis that they were truths that did not contradict one another.[16] Claiming this harmonisation was unorthodox, as it argued that in addition to revelation, the principles of *sharī'a* could also be discovered and affirmed through the method of Greek philosophy.

Ibn Rushd's broader intellectual project was to reconcile reason and revelation. His political thought was an extension of this approach. It argued that Islamic societies could greatly enhance their understanding of social organisation, political authority, and effective governance by incorporating the practical wisdom and theoretical insights found in the extra-Islamic tradition of Greek thought. In Ibn Rushd's political thought, reason served as the key point of convergence between the Islamic and Greek philosophical traditions. By demonstrating the compatibility of Greek thought with *sharī'a*, Ibn Rushd attempted to make a case for the primacy of the Aristotelean philosophical method as a means of attaining religious truth. Moreover, by establishing this harmonisation, I clarify how Ibn Rushd was able to seamlessly incorporate Greek political concepts such as the philosopher-king, the hierarchical ordering of society, and the cultivation of virtue through education within his pluralistic framework.

Ibn Rushd lived under the rule of the Almohads (Almuwahhids), a politico-religious movement originating in North Africa. Their founder, Muhammed Ibn Tumart, created an expansive territorial empire that stretched from West Africa to Spain. Almohadism propagated a new reformist version of Islam by abandoning the strictures of Islamic jurisprudence in favour of a literalist interpretation (*zāhirī*) of the Qur'an and Sunna. This proved politically challenging given the influence of a well-established network of Islamic jurists whose support was vital for the preservation of power. The official doctrine of the Almohad state thus remained wedded to the approach of Islamic jurisprudence (specifically that of Maliki *fiqh*), even if the latter were supplemented by other established approaches such as *kalām* (Islamic speculative theology) (Leaman, 1988, p. 3). Curiously, the Almohad rulers also displayed a keen interest in

---

[16] Ibn Rushd's theory of harmonisation claimed the unity of truth in both religion and philosophy. This was quite different to the 'double-truth theory' espoused by Latin Averroists in the late medieval period, which argued that truths derived from reason and philosophy could be valid and true in their own domains. For more on the double-truth theory, compare Marenbon (2007).

philosophy, which facilitated an astonishing tolerance towards its study and theoretical development. This patronage to philosophy proved crucial for Ibn Rushd, who, having been instructed by Caliph Abu Ya'qub Yusuf to simplify the books of philosophy, embarked on a lifelong project to summarise and reconcile the works of Aristotle with Islamic precepts. At the same time, Ibn Rushd also served as an Almohad government official, holding the positions of chief judge (*qāḍī*) of Cordoba and personal physician (*ṭabīb*) to the caliph. His role as a high-ranking state official may account for his interest in developing an actual theory of government for the Islamic community.

The complex political landscape of Ibn Rushd's life was marked by power struggles, territorial fragmentation, and threats of invasion. In addition to internal and external revolts, the Almohad empire faced extraordinary challenges. The local Muslim governors (*ta'ifas*) who held semiautonomous control over their territories often contested the authority of the central government, leading to internal conflict. Meanwhile, the Christian kingdoms in the north, including Castile, Aragon, and Portugal, gradually expanded their territories, threatening Muslim occupation. The Almohad armies suffered several military defeats at the hands of these Christian powers, further eroding their political control over Muslim Spain. Ibn Rushd's project to demystify the meaning of the texts of Greek philosophy produced a large corpus of writings. These included three types of commentaries: brief annotations (*jawami*), intermediate explanations (*talkhis*), and in-depth expositions (*sharh*). The latter represented his most refined ideas, encapsulating his mature thought. Additionally, Ibn Rushd composed a text of Islamic jurisprudence and three other treatises in which he harmonised religion and philosophy in an attempt to disprove the charges of heresy and disbelief laid at the door of philosophy by some Islamic jurists and theologians.

Ibn Rushd's assessment of the political world around him is a recurrent theme in his writings. He laments the poor state of governance, the lack of virtuous authority, and the inability of religious scholars to guide political affairs. He expresses this in terms of a medical analogy that likens the ideal or virtuous state to a body with well-functioning parts: 'for the hand or the foot, for example, exists only for the body as a whole, not the body for the sake of its limbs. However, the opposite is the case for these cities' (Ibn Rushd, 1974, p. 43). The principles for organising and governing an ordered society, he observes, were absent in his society because the state had 'desperately assembled territories together for its preservation' (Ibn Rushd, 1974, p. 43). In Ibn Rushd's analysis of Plato's categories of governance, he marshals an even more direct critique of contemporary forms of Islamic governance. These states, he argues, transition from virtuous government to timocracy and hedonism in a matter of generations, as demonstrated by the recent history of Muslim Spain (Ibn Rushd, 1974, pp. 104–110). He illustrates this by citing the rule of the Almoravids who had allowed the love of wealth to erode their ability to govern by virtue (Ibn Rushd, 1974, p. 125). For Ibn Rushd, virtuous governance resembled Plato's state but was guided by the principles of *sharī'a*.

Sharī'a and the Mediation of Islamic Ethics and Politics

Ibn Rushd's theory of Islamic ethics is distinctly philosophical in the form of its argument yet draws heavily from Qur'anic precepts to support its claims. In many of Ibn Rushd's writings, *sharī'a* is synonymous with the Qur'an to emphasise its divine and uncontested moral authority. For Ibn Rushd, the Qur'an contained the whole of the knowledge of the content of morality in the most perfect form possible. The Qur'an was a product of divine inspiration (*wahy*) acquired prophetically through a miraculous event (Ibn Rushd, 1954, p. 359). Ibn Rushd's key departure from the Islamic orthodoxy of his time was to claim that while the specific content of the Qur'an could only be accessed through divine revelation, the underlying principles of these commandments could be discovered and independently affirmed through human reasoning. This argument has important implications for Ibn Rushd's political project. The latter proposed that while *sharī'a* provides moral guidance for ethical living, its underlying principles harmoniously align with the goals of Greek philosophy both in aims and in purpose: 'it is evident that, the good, the bad, the useful, the harmful, the beautiful, and the base are something existing by nature, not by convention ... This is clear from these Laws and particularly this Law of ours' (Ibn Rushd, 1974, p. 81).

Ibn Rushd's pluralistic framework mediates Islamic ethics and politics by harmonising *sharī'a* with the political arguments and philosophic ethics of Plato and Aristotle. Such a mediation is underpinned by two philosophical claims: the indispensability of human reason and the idea that the Qur'an and Greek philosophy were united in their ethical objectives. Ibn Rushd's first claim contends that rational inquiry is an essential and obligatory component of Islamic ethics: 'if the activity of philosophy is nothing more than study of existing beings and reflections on them as indications of the Artisan ... and the *sharī'a*, has encouraged and urged reflections on beings, it necessarily follows that the *sharī'a*, commands this study' (Ibn Rushd, 1961, p. 44).[17] Ibn

---

[17] The Arabic word used here is شريعة. (*sharī'a*), translated as law. While we understand this term to have a broader meaning, the object of this text was to demonstrate to the juristic class that the scriptural law of Islam does not prohibit the study of philosophy by Muslims, but contrastingly makes it a duty for a certain class with the capacity to engage in demonstrative reasoning. As such, in this text the term *sharī'a* is invoked by Ibn Rushd with a more precise meaning (see Hourani, 1961, p. 1).

Rushd then supplemented this argument with a second provocative claim – that what is morally right as determined by scripture can also be known and confirmed by rational proof: 'for truth does not oppose truth but accords with it and bears witness to it' (Ibn Rushd, 1961, p. 50). These claims provided Ibn Rushd with a wide degree of latitude in ethical and political inquiry. It enabled him to fuse *sharī'a* with Aristotle's account of virtue and vice on the one hand and Plato's conception of a hierarchically ordered state governed by a guardian class with a philosopher-king on the other.

While Ibn Rushd acknowledged the role of *sharī'a* in guiding the moral actions of the political community, he did not rely solely on scriptural tenets to develop his theory of a just and well-ordered government. Instead, he sought to highlight the fundamental compatibility between *sharī'a* and Greek ethics. For Ibn Rushd, Islamic law was a code of directives towards the finer qualities of human behaviour, a manifestation of the four qualities of generosity, courage, modesty and justice' (Ibn Rushd, 1974, p. 572). Ibn Rushd's inclusion of this statement in the concluding portion of his extensive legal work[18], where he discusses the primary sources of Islamic law, is noteworthy, as it demonstrates his conviction that the principles of *sharī'a* are consistent with the key virtues recognised in Greek philosophical ethics. In his theory of Islamic politics, Ibn Rushd paid less attention to the caliphate or the prophetic model of governance in the early period of Islam. Instead, he drew upon Aristotelian concepts to justify the existence of the state and turned to Platonic ideas to define political authority. It is true that Ibn Rushd was not the first Muslim thinker to engage with Greek philosophy and Aristotelian thought. Preceding him by two centuries, Al-Kindi, Ibn Sina, and Al-Farabi had extensively explored the extra-Islamic tradition of Greek thought. Thus, Ibn Rushd was building upon a well-established legacy of philosophical engagement when he developed his own theoretical ideas.

Yet what distinguished Ibn Rushd's approach from that of his Islamic predecessors was his articulation of a comprehensive methodological framework that both emphasised the harmonisation of *sharī'a* and Greek thought and advocated for a pluralistic method in mediating Islamic ethics and politics. This methodological statement contained in a text called *The Decisive Treatise* was perceived as an affront to the prevailing religious norms of his time, which were primarily shaped by the dominant methods of Islamic theology (*kalām*) and legal science (*usūl al-fiqh*). Ibn Rushd's radical claims for incorporating the Aristotelian method in understanding the Qur'an antagonised his contemporaries, who favoured more traditional methods, such as Islamic jurisprudence, Arabic grammar, and Islamic

---

[18] Ibn Rushd's legal treatise, *The Distinguished Jurist's Primer: Bidāyat al-Mujtahid*, is widely consulted by Muslim scholars as an important legal text of Maliki jurisprudence until the present day.

theology, for such a crucial and sensitive endeavour. As Leaman suggests, the conflict around Islamic ethics in premodern Islam was thus less about propositions and more about methodology (Leaman, 1988, p. 7). In his defence of this project, Ibn Rushd claimed that the foreign nature of philosophy should not be resented, as it is the best and most reliable way to discover moral truth (Ibn Rushd, 1961, p. 43).

Ibn Rushd's *The Decisive Treatise*, written between 1178 and 1180, is known in the medieval Islamic literary genre as *Jam'Bayna*, as it seeks to reconcile seemingly conflicting ideas, opinions, or legal rulings by finding a synthesis or compromise between different viewpoints. Hourani (1961, p. 6) considers *The Decisive Treatise* the most rigorous attempt of such a unification of religion and philosophy in the premodern Islamic world. The main aim of the *The Decisive Treatise* was to defend the compatibility of reason and revelation vis-à-vis legal scholars of the time who were suspicious of philosophy. As such, this text furnishes a robust legal argument in favour of Greek philosophy, whose study, Ibn Rushd suggests, is 'obligatory' for anyone seriously concerned with the norms outlined in scripture (Ibn Rushd, 1961, p. 44). In this treatise, Ibn Rushd clarifies the utility of logical methods for discovering moral truths and interpreting *sharī'a*. Reason and intellect, he surmised, ought to be utilised in understanding religious texts to arrive at a comprehensive understanding of the truth. This rational study of *sharī'a* enhances its meaning and contributes to a more profound awareness of its truths. As such, Ibn Rushd argued:

> Whoever forbids the study of them [the methods of Greek philosophy] to anyone who is fit to study them – that is, anyone who unites two qualities – (1) natural intelligence and (2) legal integrity and moral virtue – blocks people from the door by which the Law summons them to knowledge of God, the door of theoretical study that leads to the truest knowledge of Him. (Ibn Rushd, 1961, p. 48)

The Decisive Treatise asserts that the Qur'an directs its adherents (through education and training) to undertake a study of religion using methods akin to those employed in Aristotelian philosophy. Ibn Rushd cites the authority of scripture in his defence, pointing to verses such as 'Reflect [oh] you who have vision', which affirm the significance of individual human reason and urge Muslims to contemplate and acquire knowledge through rational reflection (Ibn Rushd, 1961, p. 45). However, the Qur'an does not explicitly declare Greek philosophy or rational inquiry as prerequisites for attaining religious understanding, a critique potentially levelled at Ibn Rushd's argument (Omar, 2019, p. 8). Ibn Rushd maintains that drawing on the ideas, methods, and concepts of ancient traditions is not in conflict with Islamic teaching but rather a legitimate and mandatory Islamic endeavour: 'everything that is required in the study of the subject of intellectual syllogisms has already been examined in the most perfect manner by the ancients, presumably we ought to lay hands on their books in order to study what they said about that subject' (Ibn Rushd, 1961, p. 47). According to Ibn Rushd, it is Aristotle who provides the intellectual resources for determining truth through his method of demonstrative reasoning: 'demonstrative proof which affords necessary, absolute truth must be distinguished from dialectical and rhetorical proofs which only yield probability' (Ibn Rushd, 1954, p. 1). The conclusions reached through demonstrative reasoning, Ibn Rushd surmised, were certain and indisputable, as they are based on the necessity of logical inference. For Ibn Rushd, Aristotle was venerated as the 'first master' and 'philosopher of truth'.[19]

In his pluralistic framework, Ibn Rushd places particular emphasis on the role of reason in achieving a harmonisation between the extra-Islamic tradition of Greek thought and *sharī'a*. He asserts that when confronted with ambiguity in scripture, reason, in the form of allegorical interpretation, becomes an indispensable supplement to revelation (Ibn Rushd, 1961, pp. 51–52). For Ibn Rushd, allegorical interpretation (*ta'wīl*) involves going beyond the literal meaning of the scriptural text to uncover deeper, hidden meanings that are compatible with reason and demonstrative truths. This process requires interpreting metaphorical or ambiguous passages in a way that aligns with Aristotelian logical principles. This determination was largely at odds with al-Ghazali's earlier formulation which defined the criterion for allegorical interpretation by declaring that the Qur'an should be understood in its literal sense except when it may contradict another verse and that some verses like those on the afterlife could not be subject to rational investigation (Di Giovanni, 2018, p. 18). Ibn Rushd was not satisfied with these impositions on reason in interpreting scripture, despite his agreement with al-Ghazali on the danger of the proliferation of arbitrary opinions on the meaning of the Qur'an. He proceeded to formulate his own criterion for Islamic interpretative inquiry by outlining four categories of dealing with scripture:

> The first is that whose representation is given [in scripture], but whose existence is only known through lengthy and complex syllogisms that are learnt over a long period of time and through various arts and are not understood except by people of superior natures ... The second part is the opposite of the [first]. Here the two cases are known relatively easily ... The third part is when it is known readily to be a representation of the thing in question and why, in an elaborate way ... The fourth is the opposite of this, where it is known readily why it is a representation, but with difficulty that it is a representation. (Ibn Rushd, 2001, p. 131)

---

[19] This is evident in Ibn Rushd's tendency to understand (and even disagree with) Plato through Aristotle: 'if this be the correct opinion, Plato does not favour it; but it is Aristotle's opinion, and it is the indubitable truth' (Ibn Rushd, 1974, p. 46).

Ibn Rushd's crucial theological innovation here was to argue that the verses of scripture ranged from extremely complex and abstruse to very straightforward, and that allegorical interpretation of scripture's complex aspects should accordingly be undertaken by a select group of trained philosophers with the skills in applying reason to determine its meaning: 'The reason why we have received in Scripture texts whose apparent meanings contradict each other is in order to draw the attention of those who are well grounded in science to the interpretation which reconciles them' (Ibn Rushd, 1961, p. 50).[20] Disclosing the hidden meanings of scripture on theoretical matters to all people would be impossible and even dangerous, as these 'matters of doctrine' are likely to violate Islamic consensus (Ibn Rushd, 1961, p. 53). In contrast, he maintains that the hidden meanings related to practical matters, which concern action, should be disclosed to everyone to establish unanimity within the political community (Ibn Rushd, 1961, p. 53). Moreover, he argues that when the authority to interpret scriptures fell into the hands of those who could not properly distinguish between the different contexts and audiences that various passages were intended for, it led to widespread confusion and misunderstanding (Ibn Rushd, 2001, p. 131). As a result, many divergent sects emerged, each accusing the others of being unbelievers based on their differing interpretations. This situation amounted to a fundamental ignorance of the true intended meaning behind the scriptures, essentially violating their original political purpose and intent (Ibn Rushd, 2001, p. 131). While framed as a theological critique, Ibn Rushd is making a pointed political statement about curbing the monopoly of religious authorities in determining the meaning of Islam, in order to reduce the destabilising effects of sectarian conflict. He is also implicitly making a case for the importance of pursuing a more rational-based Islamic orthodoxy grounded in demonstrative reason.

Ibn Rushd's insistence on the primacy of human reason constitutes a bold attempt to address the central methodological question of ethical theology: what methods not mentioned in scripture are men authorised to use (if ever) to determine doctrine? (Hourani, 1985, p. 271). Theologians and jurists felt obligated to justify their use of reason as either derived from or at least not contradicting *sharī'a*. *The Decisive Treatise* satisfies the latter condition through a central premise of Ibn Rushd's pluralistic framework: the unity of purpose (*telos*). According to this premise, religion and philosophy teach the

---

[20] Practical matters, in Ibn Rushd's view, encompass issues of ethics, politics, and human conduct. The latter concern how individuals should act in the world and make moral and political decisions. Theoretical matters, on the other hand, are matters of abstract and speculative knowledge. They include metaphysical, philosophical, and scientific inquiries into the nature of reality, the cosmos, and the fundamental principles of existence.

same truth in different ways, without any double truth or contradiction in their message. As a result, Ibn Rushd grants human reason unprecedented power to discover Islamic moral truths by incorporating the extra-Islamic tradition of the Greek philosophical method.

Islamic Ethics: Virtue, Happiness, and the Objectivity of Values

Ibn Rushd's theory of Islamic ethics combines 'theoretical' and 'practical' arguments. The theoretical arguments, interlaced with Aristotelian natural philosophy and metaphysics, are especially complex and emphasise his more controversial views on the necessity of causality, the denial of the immortality of the soul, and the distinction between essence and existence (Ibn Rushd, 1954). While Ibn Rushd defends these arguments with doctrinal proof, this aspect of his thought has invited interpretations that cast doubt on his fidelity to religion.[21] On the other hand, the 'practical' arguments of his ideas focus on less abstract concepts and are concerned with 'voluntary actions', virtue and the question of politics and governance (Ibn Rushd, 1974, p. 7). Following Aristotle, for Ibn Rushd, ethics, as the prologue to politics, concerns the relationship between habits and volitional actions. Politics considers how these habits are established in the soul and how they are able to attain perfection in the context of a state (Ibn Rushd, 1974, p. 4).

Ibn Rushd's conception of Islamic ethics was markedly influenced by Plato and Aristotle insofar as he upheld the objectivity of values. He argued that scriptural commandments are objectively right: 'it is evident that, the good, the bad, the useful, the harmful, the beautiful, and the base are something existing by nature, not by convention' (Ibn Rushd, 1974, p. 81). This question of the objectivity of values was a source of major disagreement in premodern Islamic ethical debates. This debate centred on whether values exist independently of human perception and belief or are subjective constructs dependent on scriptural authority (Hourani, 1985, pp. 1–5). The Mu'tazilite school argued for the inherent objectivity of values, which could be discovered through reason and/or scripture, while the Ash'arite school, influenced by Al-Ghazali, maintained that values align with God's commands and can only be known through tradition, with reason playing a merely supplementary role (Hourani, 1985, pp. 1–5). This latter view, termed 'ethical voluntarism' or 'theistic subjectivism', held significant sway among traditionalist theologians and jurists. In contrast, Ibn Rushd advanced a third position, following Aristotle and Plato, who argued for the objectivity of values that could be apprehended entirely through the independent reasoning of

---

[21] This 'Straussian' interpretation is based on two assumptions: first, that Ibn Rushd worked in a hostile environment and was obliged to represent his views as being in conformity with Islam; and, second, that he had to present his real philosophical views in disguise (Gutas, 2002, p. 20).

The Pluralistic Frameworks

philosophers. Here, Ibn Rushd's theological innovation lay in his assertion that these objective values were communicated to the masses by prophets using the language of scriptural tradition. This move allowed him to reconcile the ethical contradiction faced by earlier Muslim philosophers who prioritised reason over revelation by claiming that both sources of ethics were united in the ultimate purpose of affirming truth.

Ibn Rushd's approach to Islamic ethics, I suggest, was thus unorthodox in its emphasis on the role of human reason in apprehending objective moral truths. While earlier Muslim philosophers also championed the primacy of reason, Ibn Rushd's argument that the truths of revelation could be fully comprehended and affirmed by philosophical inquiry was a bold and controversial claim in the context of Islamic intellectual history. Following Aristotle, he contends that there is a universal account of well-being grounded in human nature. Virtues are dispositions, engendered by education or habituation, to act by standards of moral excellence (Ibn Rushd, 1974, p. 5). The ultimate aim (*ghāya*) of human existence is to attain happiness (*sa'āda*) by actualising the potential of the intellect through the cultivation of theoretical and practical virtue. Ethics and politics thus have an end goal or purpose (*telos*), namely happiness (*as-sa'ada*), which depends on the inculcation of virtue: 'right practice consists in performing the acts which bring happiness and avoiding the acts which bring misery' (Ibn Rushd, 1961, p. 63).

Ibn Rushd's philosophical conception of Islamic ethics oriented towards virtue and happiness implicitly challenges the voluntarist view adopted by some Ash'arī theologians, who held that good and evil are entirely dependent on God's will. He affirms the objectivity of moral values while insisting on their ultimate compatibility with revelation. Ibn Rushd identifies three main approaches to ethics in the Islamic world corresponding to different levels of human understanding: (1) demonstration (*burhān*), which is the preservation of the philosophers; (2) dialectic (*jadal*), employed by the theologians; and (3) rhetoric (*khiṭāb*), used by the jurists and preachers to instruct the masses. While all three methods can lead to the truth, demonstration alone yields certain knowledge. Dialectic produces mere opinion, while rhetoric persuades people without providing real understanding (Ibn Rushd, 2001, p. 77). The philosophers, qualified in the art of demonstrative reasoning, were thus in his view uniquely qualified to guide the community towards virtue. Ibn Rushd's conception of Islamic ethics thus constitutes a powerful synthesis of Aristotelian virtue ethics and Islamic piety, emphasising the cultivation of character through the perfection of reason. The philosopher's pursuit of theoretical and practical wisdom represents the highest form of worship, a spiritual endeavour that fulfils the deepest aspirations of *sharī'a*.

Ibn Rushd's unified conception of ethics has important implications for his account of politics. This can be explained in two parts. The first part suggested that the purpose of *sharīʿa* was political and ethical – to prescribe laws and rules that can be commonly accepted in a society to promote virtuous ends. These laws and rules, by dint of their divine nature, were the surest way of inciting the political community to virtuous action (Ibn Rushd, 1954, p. 361). Religious laws were thus 'necessary political arts' (Ibn Rushd, 1954, p. 359). Happiness through the cultivation of moral virtue and obedience to *sharīʿa* was the ultimate purpose of politics: '[i]t is this very Law that motivates and calls us towards the ultimate happiness' (Ibn Rushd, 1961, p. 49). The role of government is to engender virtuous ends in accordance with *sharīʿa*. Those brought up on the tenets of religion, he surmised, are more perfect in virtue than their counterparts; for example, the daily ritual of Islamic prayers prevents the political community from succumbing to wickedness and ignominy (Ibn Rushd, 1954, p. 361). Ibn Rushd's ideal state was therefore virtuous to the extent that it was capable of instilling moral education in the political community. Ethics and politics were thus intertwined in an unconventional and fascinating interpolation of Greek philosophy and *sharīʿa*.

The Ideal Islamic State: Plato and *Sharīʿa*

As a philosopher who undertook, in a substantive way, the revival of Aristotelian thought, Ibn Rushd lamented the lack of availability of Aristotle's *Politics*, turning instead to Plato's *Republic* to formulate a theory of government.[22] In his effort to theorise politics, Ibn Rushd thus draws on both Platonic and Aristotelian ideas and combines them in an intriguing way. He begins by drawing from Aristotle's *Nicomachean Ethics* (rather than the Qur'an) the types of human perfection (theoretical and intellectual, moral and practical) that constitute virtue (Ibn Rushd, 1974, p. 5). It is fitting, he argues, for every person 'to obtain as many human perfections as are compatible with their individual nature' (Ibn Rushd, 1974, p. 10). Following Aristotle, Ibn Rushd argues that there is a universal account of well-being grounded in human nature, something akin to natural law. Ostensibly this raises an interesting discussion about the philosophical place of natural law in the Islamic tradition, given that the source of moral obligation is typically considered to be God, as derived from divine law.[23] Ibn Rushd, for

---

[22] Ibn Rushd states that he did not have access to a copy of Aristotle's *Politics*: 'and also in this book of Plato that we intend to explain since Aristotle's book on politics has not yet fallen into our hands' (Ibn Rushd, 1974, p. 4).

[23] Recent scholarship has highlighted the presence of natural law theories in both the Islamic jurisprudential and philosophical traditions. Enver Emon (2010), for example, provides textual justification for a tradition of natural law in the legal theory of premodern Muslim jurists, distinguishing between 'hard naturalists', who granted ontological authority to reason in their treatment of *sharīʿa*, and 'soft naturalists', who argued that rational reasoning alone cannot

example, makes reference to an 'unwritten law', which can be understood as a theory of natural law mediating between divine and human law (Taliaferro, 2017, p. 22). The basic point here is that we may understand Ibn Rushd's conception of natural law as situated within a broader Islamic intellectual tradition, where the relationship between reason and revelation was a central concern. By drawing on both Platonic and Aristotelian ideas, he sought to develop a political theory that recognised a form of Aristotelian natural law, while navigating the complexities of Islamic theology and jurisprudence. This was certainly another notable feature of his pluralistic framework.

Ibn Rushd's ideal state respects the natural order among virtues and practical arts. In its organisation and administration, the state must mirror the natural order of virtues in the individual soul to ensure a perfect political community (Butterworth, 2004, p. 282). Governments fail when they neglect the proper hierarchy of human virtues or pursue an errant end (Butterworth, 2004, p. 282). Ethics and politics thus have an end goal or purpose (*telos*), namely the happiness of the entire political community. Happiness depends on the inculcation of virtue or right practices: 'right practice consists in performing the acts which bring happiness and avoiding the acts which bring misery' (Ibn Rushd, 1961, p. 63). Ibn Rushd conceives of virtues as dispositions, engendered by education or habituation, to act by standards of moral excellence (Ibn Rushd, 1974, p. 5).

The origins of government in Ibn Rushd's political thought are also distinctly Aristotelian. The purpose of the state is not simply to fulfil human perfection but to realise basic and everyday needs 'such as appropriating food, securing dwelling places and clothing, and generally anything that man is in need of, because of the appetitive or vital faculties within him' (Ibn Rushd, 1974, p. 5). Human beings are political by nature, and to acquire virtue, each individual stands in need of others (Ibn Rushd, 1974, p. 5). With respect to Plato's model of virtuous governance, Ibn Rushd constructed a hierarchical system based on the natural division of labour and the specialisation of classes. In Ibn Rushd's ideal state, 'not every man is fit to be a warrior, an orator or a poet, let alone a philosopher' (Ibn Rushd, 1974, p. 6). The state ought to rank groups in the correct order of status, from a lower artisan and producing class, to a higher guardian class containing philosophers capable of ruling. Without such ordering, happiness will not be achieved: 'human virtues will not be attained at all or their attainment will be defective' (Ibn Rushd, 1974, p. 7). This epistemological theory of classes views Islamic political society through a Platonic lens rather than a Qur'anic lens (Black, 2001, p. 118).

---

render a norm authoritative in *sharī'a*. Al-Ghazali and Al-Shatibi, both soft naturalists, developed theories of natural reasoning that fused fact and value in nature through the concept of *maslaha* (public interest), while maintaining the ultimate authority of divine omnipotence.

As such, the particular features of Plato's account of virtuous governance that Ibn Rushd appropriates include two important ideas. The first idea is that humans are naturally divided into distinct classes by the preordained function (ruling/fighting/trading) for which they are suited. Ibn Rushd defends Plato's reasoning for the existence of this division of classes as follows:

> [a] Because of an unavoidable necessity (e.g., it is impossible for an isolated man to secure what he needs by way of food, housing and clothing); [b] because it is easier (e.g., it is possible for Zayd not to till the soil and sow seeds, but if he tills and sows [with a view to others' needs too], he will live at greater ease); or [c] because it is the best way, for if a man has chosen an art since his early youth and has practised it for a long time, his performance in that art will be better. (Ibn Rushd, 1974, pp. 5–6)

The second idea that Ibn Rushd acquires from Plato's theory of virtuous governance is that there are four virtues (wisdom, courage, temperance, justice) and that a just state is one in which the four virtues are as well cultivated as possible (Ibn Rushd, 1974, p. 7). Following Plato, Ibn Rushd argues that both of these ideas are linked in that virtue in a state will be best cultivated if everyone has been given a job corresponding to the type of function to which they are naturally suited. Ibn Rushd determined that it is consistent to employ Plato's hierarchical conception of political society and to argue that it is from *sharī'a* that one finds the best articulation of what these virtues consist of or imply for Muslim public life. Unsurprisingly, the first of these ideas is contrary to human equality; that is, one's status in life is dictated by one's natural talent. Since for Plato there is no social mobility and one station is more noble or higher than the other stations, the price of combining *sharī'a* and Plato in this way would be a tacit admission in which *sharī'a* is consistent with the idea of human inequality. The implications of this last point are ambiguous and not clearly addressed in Ibn Rushd's political writings, although they are contrary to those of the Qur'an.

In Ibn Rushd's assessment of Plato's criteria for selecting the leader among the guardian class, he emphasises the love for the welfare of the political community along with discipline (Ibn Rushd, 1974, p. 34). Ibn Rushd suggests that individuals with such qualities are like 'gold refined in fire' and should be trained to govern and protect the state effectively (Ibn Rushd, 1974, p. 35). He underscores Plato's belief in the significance of education and training, outlining four conditions that the philosopher-king must meet: the ability to discover and teach theoretical sciences, wisdom in practical science, cogitative virtue, and great moral virtue (Ibn Rushd, 1974, p. 71). The other attributes cannot be learned and are presented as natural, arising from the dominance of reason in the soul. They include all of the

The Pluralistic Frameworks 33

attributes emphasised by Plato: love of knowledge, distinctiveness, truthfulness, retentiveness of memory, courage, the despising of sensual desires, and relinquishing the love of wealth (Ibn Rushd, 1974, pp. 73–75). Ibn Rushd (1974, p. 75) adds eloquence in speech to this list because the ideal Islamic ruler must be able to interpret and teach the *sharī'a* at the appropriate level of understanding. Such a blending and synthesisation of Islamic and Greek ideas is indicative of his pluralistic approach.

Ibn Rushd's pluralistic approach is also apparent in his account of the virtuous qualities of the ideal Islamic ruler. These qualities include practical wisdom, intelligence, persuasion, imagination, military ability (for *jihād*), and freedom from physical defects (Ibn Rushd, 1974, p. 106). The latter two are clearly influenced by the conventions of the Islamic political tradition in that they represent the traditional qualities of the caliph (Hourani, 1985, p. 267). By combining traditional and philosophical virtues, Ibn Rushd is able to equate Plato's philosopher-king with the Islamic idea of a lawgiver or imam. He supports this alignment by asserting that the term 'imam' signifies 'one who is followed in his actions', a quality shared with the philosopher: 'He who is followed in these actions by which he is a philosopher, is an Imam in the absolute sense' (Ibn Rushd, 1974, p. 72). Ultimately, for Ibn Rushd, the philosopher-king/imam should possess knowledge of both philosophy and Islamic jurisprudence (*fiqh*).

In his ideal Islamic state, Ibn Rushd identifies two primary methods for cultivating virtue in the political community: education and coercion. Education, the first and most important method, is the responsibility of the ruler, who must teach people wisdom and the truths of *sharī'a*. Ibn Rushd argues that the guidelines for teaching virtue are already outlined in the Qur'an, which addresses the different levels of understanding among people: 'for the natures of men are on different levels with respect to [their paths to] assent. One of them comes to assent through demonstration; another comes to assent through dialectical arguments . . . since his nature does not contain any greater capacity, while another comes to assent through rhetorical arguments' (Ibn Rushd, 1961, p. 49). To be politically effective, *sharī'a* must appeal to a diverse cross-section of people, each possessing their own distinctive capacity to comprehend its laws. Ibn Rushd compares the purpose of *sharī'a* to that of a doctor who aims 'to preserve the health and cure the diseases of all the people, by prescribing for them rules which can be commonly accepted' (Ibn Rushd, 1974, p. 22). He places significant emphasis on the persuasive language and imagery of the Qur'an, which although varied in linguistic expression and reasoning, conveys a consistent moral and ethical message.

The second method of instilling virtue, coercion, is reserved for non-virtuous polities and is not recommended by Ibn Rushd for an ideal Islamic state. He criticises states that govern through harsh punishments such as castigation, disgrace, flogging, and execution, describing them as bad (Ibn Rushd, 1974, p. 11). In contrast, *sharī'a* promotes virtue primarily through speech and persuasion, limiting coercion to waging war against obdurate nations. In his *Middle Commentary on Nicomachean Ethics* (1177), Ibn Rushd presents a pluralistic notion of just war theory by referencing Aristotle's definition of equity, which serves to rectify flawed laws that are excessively general (see Berman, 1967). To illustrate this concept, he examines the question of *jihād* from the perspective of *sharī'a*, which often states a general mandate for perpetual warfare against all non-Muslim nations (cited in Hourani, 1985, p. 268). In response, Ibn Rushd notes that Muslims have suffered significantly due to this overly broad interpretation and suggests, following Aristotle's principle of equity, that peace should generally be preferred, with war being the exception (cited in Hourani, 1985, p. 269).

Ibn Rushd was convinced by the moral authority of *sharī'a*, given its prophetically revealed nature. This belief in the divine nature of revelation was an article of faith that shaped his political thought and determined his mode of expression (Rosenthal, 1956, p. 8).[24] In the *Exposition of the Methods of Proof concerning Religious Argument* (1179/1180), Ibn Rushd adduces the miraculous nature of the Qur'an by pointing to the ingenuity of its theoretical and practical prescriptions, the confirmation of its predications, and its unmatched literary excellence (Ibn Rushd, 2001, pp. 100–101). Islam, he surmises, was 'intended for all mankind ... because of the universality of the teaching of the Precious Book [Qur'an] and the universality of the laws contained in it' (Ibn Rushd, 2001, p. 103). Throughout his works, Ibn Rushd assertively proclaimed his commitment to faith and reason. The mission of the Prophet Muhammad as the lawgiver was to 'instruct' the 'common people' and the 'learned' 'according to their rational capacities' (Ibn Rushd, 2001, p. 77).

It is true that Ibn Rushd considered Plato's political teaching valid for Muslims and deemed its actualisation a genuine prospect (Lerner, 1974, p. xxviii). As such, he declared Plato's regime the 'quickest, easiest and best' model for Islamic political reform (Ibn Rushd, 1974, p. 79). The Qur'an did not preclude this possibility (even though Ibn Rushd does not address the point of human inequality as stated earlier in this Element). Indeed, Ibn Rushd was at pains to show that Plato's model of governance offered all of the necessary normative prescriptions for perfecting the virtues contained in the *sharī'a*. The success of Plato's model, however, depended on the correct interpretation of *sharī'a* and the political

---

[24] Again, Leo Strauss' (1988) claim in *Persecution and the Art of Writing* that Muslim philosophers like Ibn Rushd offered esoteric interpretations of some of their most radical ideas to avoid theological censure is unfounded, and at best dubious. The idea that Ibn Rushd engaged in a kind of 'double discourse' to avoid political persecution fails to take seriously the sincerity of his beliefs. The sometimes recondite, obscure, and enigmatic aspects of his thought do not presuppose a hidden political agenda; Ibn Rushd made apparent his enduring desire to harmonise faith and reason.

judgement of an ideal ruler. An imam, as a philosopher-king skilled in oratory, would exercise political judgement to convey the meaning of religious law at the appropriate level of understanding (Ibn Rushd, 1974, p. 61).

Two fascinating aspects of Ibn Rushd's theory of politics concern women and property. Regarding the former, he cites Plato's analogy of the skilled female dog and his own example of the desert women of Daghuda to argue for the possibility of women philosophers and rulers (Ibn Rushd, 1974, p. 58).[25] Ibn Rushd draws on this analogy to make a similar argument about the potential of women to contribute to the intellectual and political life of the state. He observes that in his own society, women are confined to the domestic sphere and to the activities of procreation and child-rearing, depriving them of educational opportunities, which he sees as a waste of human potential and a cause of the poverty of the state (Ibn Rushd, 1974, p. 97). By citing the example of the desert women of Daghuda, who presumably enjoyed greater freedom and participation in social and economic life, Ibn Rushd suggests that women are capable of much more than the roles assigned to them in his society . In Ibn Rushd's (2000) legal compendium, many of the juridical positions he advances regarding women's prayer and property concur with his reading of Plato's political theory (Belo, 2022).

On the question of property, Plato proposed that those in positions of political authority should dissolve their private households and abstain from accumulating personal wealth. Building upon Plato's ideas, Ibn Rushd argues against property ownership for rulers, stating that it is the cause of conflict, corruption, and greed (Ibn Rushd, 1974, p. 38). Observing his own context, he remarks that greed in acquiring private property results in extravagant rulers and corrupt elites who arouse the community's enmity and hatred (Ibn Rushd, 1974, p. 39). Ibn Rushd contends that while some might view wealth as a virtue, it does not constitute a form of virtue that rulers should adopt (Ibn Rushd, 1974, p. 40). Significantly, both examples are illustrative of Ibn Rushd's pluralistic framework, which uses reason to adapt and reformulate Plato's political thought to foreground the *sharī'a*'s alignment with the participation of women in the political realm and the importance of economic justice. It also remains uncertain whether Ibn Rushd would have given serious consideration to these ideas had he not presented them as part of his larger project of engaging with and adapting Plato's political philosophy.

---

[25] In Plato's *Republic*, Socrates uses the analogy of a skilled female dog to argue that women should be given the same opportunities as men in the guardian class of the ideal city. Socrates extends the analogy to the guardian class, arguing that just as female dogs can excel at hunting alongside male dogs, so too can women excel in the same pursuits as men, including philosophy and ruling the city, if given the proper education and training (Plato, Book V, 451d–e).

Practical Wisdom and Islamic Political Authority

Ibn Rushd's emphasis on Aristotelean practical wisdom as a key virtue of Islamic political authority is crucial for understanding his pluralistic framework and his project of rethinking politics. Like Aristotle, Ibn Rushd argues that practical wisdom, acquired through years of theoretical education and possessed only by a select group of philosophers, is indispensable for governing a city, as it is the intellectual virtue concerned with moral judgement. Ibn Rushd's ideal virtuous state rests on a philosopher-king/imam who directly exercises moral judgement (practical wisdom) to deduce the meaning of law. This ideal Islamic ruler has a special juridical insight with respect to *sharī'a* (Rosenthal, 1953, p. 259), which is derived from his ability to engage in demonstrative reason. By granting the philosopher a higher political status than the jurist or theologian, Ibn Rushd's account of the ideal Islamic ruler implies the superiority of philosophy – the method of the ancient Greeks – over the methods previously devised by pious Muslims for determining what is right and virtuous in a political community. Given Islamic political thought that the Islamic ruler should be versed in religious knowledge, Ibn Rushd's position was unorthodox in arguing for a ruler to have special knowledge of religious affairs derived philosophically. This may explain why Ibn Rushd placed greater emphasis on the state's role in developing virtue than either Aristotle or the Muslim philosophers preceding him (Black, 2001, p. 121). Ultimately, for Ibn Rushd, the ideal Islamic state guided by the ruler's practical wisdom was to ensure the prevalence of the right kind of moral decision-making while maintaining political stability and order.

Ibn Rushd's pluralistic synthesis of the philosopher-king/imam is also interesting for thinking about the question of true religious knowledge (*ilm*) and its separation from the conventional sites of power and authority vested in Islamic theologians and jurists. Here, Ibn Rushd contends that Islamic jurists, caught up in worldly affairs, lack the intellectual virtue of practical wisdom required for applying *sharī'a* to practical political situations (Ibn Rushd, 1961, p. 49). Moreover, the jurist's activity 'is not the direct exercise of moral judgement (practical wisdom) but the deduction of moral decisions from scripture. This is legal reasoning or legal analogy' (Ibn Rushd, 1961, p. 50). Moral judgement can be understood as political judgement informed by practical wisdom, an art which, for Ibn Rushd, is developed through a deep knowledge of the theoretical sciences (i.e., Aristotelian philosophy). This determination reveals that, for Ibn Rushd, *sharī'a* had a political purpose which could be best managed if the philosopher was tasked with political authority. Dialectical reasoning applied by jurists used commonly accepted premises rather than principles of pure reason to guide the political community towards virtue (Hourani, 1985, p. 268). Ibn Rushd's theory of politics was therefore not simply an endorsement of rational inquiry but also a radical Aristotelian proposal for Islamic political reform that reimagined the role of *sharī'a*.

In Ibn Rushd's ideal state, those tasked with political authority must recognise the three levels of reasoning in the Qur'an – demonstrative, dialectical, and rhetorical – and call various classes within the political community to virtue by applying the appropriate level of instruction: 'summon to the way of your Lord by wisdom and by good preaching, and debate with them in the most effective manner' (Ibn Rushd, 1961, p. 49). The vast majority of people respond to moral action through rhetorical reasoning, as they are easily convinced by persuasive language and attractive imagery, which the Qur'an employs abundantly (Leaman, 1988, p. 154). In contrast, the intellectual class can uncover concealed meanings in the Qur'an through rational inquiry and demonstration, although the philosopher may choose not to disclose these meanings to those lacking the necessary capacity for comprehension (Ibn Rushd, 1961, p. 64).

One of the problems Ibn Rushd identified with the political authority of his own time was the influence of religious scholars (*ulama*) in determining political affairs, despite their lack of practical wisdom and theoretical knowledge: 'their thought and their leadership over the cities . . . is indeed the greatest of the causes for the loss of wisdom and the extinguishing of light' (Ibn Rushd, 1974, p. 74). He praises his patron Almohad Caliph Abu Ya'qub Yusuf for supporting philosophy but criticises his failure to discipline misguiding scholars (Ibn Rushd, 1961, p. 19). He also laments the condition of Muslim philosophers, whose value and practical wisdom were not properly recognised. This suggests that the ideal Islamic state envisaged by Ibn Rushd was not simply an abstract notion derived from Plato's *Republic* but a model he hoped would materialise in his own context (Rosenthal, 1953, p. 259). Ultimately, Ibn Rushd's conception of political authority and damning critiques of the jurists and theologians of his time further solidified the view of his unorthodoxy. This not only challenged the dominant theological and juridical paradigms of his time but affected him personally. By 1195, not even his patron the caliph could prevent his trial, which sentenced him to temporary exile on charges of heresy and disbelief. Consequently, the Almohad caliph Abu Yusuf Ya'qub al-Mansur condemned Ibn Rushd's philosophical works and ordered the burning of his books. Ibn Rushd was exiled to Lucena, a small town near Córdoba, and was stripped of his position as a judge and banned from teaching or engaging in public life. This banishment was likely due to political reasons, as Ibn Rushd's philosophical views had become increasingly controversial and were seen as a threat to the authority of the Almohad dynasty. The reception of Ibn Rushd's ideas during his period also elicited consternation. Notable scholars of his period accused him of heresy and of prioritising philosophical reasoning over the sacred truths of religious revelation.[26]

Finally, Ibn Rushd's pluralistic framework was not simply to produce a variety of religious arguments that could be demonstrated philosophically. His methodological approach was more careful and considered. It sought to reconcile a wide array of philosophical propositions ('theoretical' and 'practical' as discussed previously in this Element) by claiming its harmony with *sharī'a*. Such harmonisation depended on the complex use of religious and philosophical language. As Leaman suggested, the notions of 'equivocation' and 'linguistic ambiguity' must be recognised as central to his methodology (Leaman, 1988, p. 196). Following Aristotle, Ibn Rushd recognised that words could have different meanings in different contexts. The determination of whether a word or concept is ambiguous is influenced by social factors. In other words, whether something is considered ambiguous or not is not solely a matter of inherent linguistic properties but is shaped by the way that language is used and understood within a specific social and cultural context. This leads Ibn Rushd to another insight concerning equivocation as a feature of language both in religion and in the ordinary world (Leaman, 1988, p. 195). For Ibn Rushd, equivocation implies the flexibility of language in capturing a diversity of views that accord with a common truth. In his philosophical methodology, Ibn Rushd attempts to show that apparently contradictory views can be reconciled if they manifest a common truth (Leaman, 1988, p. 196). This approach was central to his mediation of Islamic ethics and politics, which sought to harmonise reason and revelation as complementary sources of truth within a pluralistic framework.

By closely engaging with Ibn Rushd's own writings and situating these ideas within the debates of his time, this section has sought to highlight the distinctiveness and originality of his political thought. Ibn Rushd's pluralistic framework, I have argued, represents a bold attempt to expand the scope of Islamic intellectual thought by incorporating the sources of Greek philosophy and reconciling its central methods and ideas with *sharī'a*. His distinctive theological innovation, asserting the compatibility of *sharī'a* with the rationalistic methods of Greek philosophy, represents a significant departure from the dominant theological and

---

[26] There is no doubt that Ibn Rushd's ideas were less influential in the centuries preceding his death as compared to other notable scholars like Ibn Sina. This was largely due to the polemical nature of Ibn Rushd's ideas and its critical reception in the Muslim world. Yet as recent studies confirm, Ibn Rushd harnessed many disciples in the East and is also admired as 'a rationalist par excellence in Islamic intellectual history' (Adamson & Giovanni, 2019, p. 7). For more on the positive contemporary reception of Ibn Rushd in the 20th century see von Kügelgen (1996).

juridical approaches of his time. By arguing for the discovery and affirmation of *sharīʿa* principles through Greek philosophical methods, Ibn Rushd opens up new possibilities for the understanding and application of Islamic ethics in the political realm. Recovering his mediating approach between Islamic ethics and politics offers a model for grappling with the complex relationship between religion and philosophy in both historical and contemporary contexts. Ibn Rushd's intellectual legacy is therefore a powerful example of the potential for pluralistic modes of thinking to enrich and transform the Islamic tradition from within. Yet it also reveals the limitations of his pluralistic approach, which embraces a form of ambiguity and flexibility that unsettles the conventional boundaries between Islamic and extra-Islamic traditions of thought by claiming a reconciliation with *sharīʿa* that does align with its traditional methods and sensibilities.

3 Negotiating *Sharīʿa* and Liberal Thought: The Pluralistic Framework of Abdullahi Ahmed An-Na'im

Sudanese Muslim political thinker and legal scholar Abdullahi Ahmed An-Nai'm (1946–) begins his treatise on Islamic political theory with the following claim: '[i]n order to be a Muslim by conviction and free choice, which is the only way one can be a Muslim, I need a secular state' (An-Na'im, 2008, p. 1). In this section, I clarify the contours of this bold and radical claim by reconstructing An-Na'im's normative account of the secular state in Islam. In my analysis, I identify the underlying assumptions which frame An-Na'im's political thought so as to better understand his mediation of Islamic ethics and politics. My central claims are that An-Na'im's pluralistic framework discloses a complex interplay between *sharīʿa* and the extra-Islamic tradition of liberal political thought and that his political project, which seeks to achieve congruence between the two, depends on an unorthodox and radical reformulation of Islamic ethics. To defend these claims, I evaluate two significant normative themes which underpin An-Na'im's pluralistic approach to Islamic politics in the modern world. The first theme is the need for a dynamic and creative development of *sharīʿa*, as the basis of a more flexible and adaptable Islamic legal system (An-Naim, 2008, pp. 9–16). The second theme is the need for a religiously neutral state which recognises and regulates the unavoidable connectedness of Islam with politics. Both these normative themes, I suggest, depend, in the first instance, on understanding An-Na'im's radical reform of Islamic law, which constitutes a departure from Islamic legal normativity and which seeks to subvert *sharīʿa* under the instruments of liberal thought.

An-Na'im's liberalising approach to *sharīʿa* is deeply rooted in his life history and political biography. Born in 1946 in Al-Magawhir, a rural village north of Khartoum, Sudan, An-Na'im spent the first ten years of his childhood under

British colonial occupation. The postcolonial state of the Republic of Sudan, established in 1956, provides the backdrop for many of the key biographical events that directly inform his writing and ideas.

Three aspects of An-Na'im's life require particular emphasis. First, his parents' early commitment to the value of education beyond religious learning and the oral tradition allowed him to question the tensions between tradition and modernity and to distinguish the importance of form versus substance in a society dominated by external religiosity and conformity. This formative educational exposure also inspired An-Na'im to pursue a post-school qualification in law, which he saw as an opportunity to help achieve a more just society. In 1970, he graduated with a degree in law from the University of Khartoum.

Second, the political context of postcolonial Sudan, marked by unremitting political turmoil, civilian and military rule, the fractures of political Islam, authoritarianism, and civil war, had a profound impact on An-Na'im's thinking. He highlights the banning of political parties (1965), Nimeiry's military coup (1969), and the Islamist takeover of government (1983) as central events that destabilised Sudan's government and state institutions. The culmination of this instability occurred in 1983 when Jaffar Nimeiry's one-party military government declared an Islamic revolution, imposing an Islamic state conceived along a narrow interpretation of *sharī'a* as state law. An-Na'im recalls that this period further intensified ethnic conflicts between Muslims in the north and Christians in the south, resulting in a civil war. This period stands out as formative in shaping the political and social cleavages in Sudanese society.

Third, An-Na'im's personal experiences of exile and incarceration shaped his intellectual and political trajectory. During this tumultuous political period in Sudan, An-Na'im sought exile abroad, travelling for further education and training. He obtained an LLB from the University of Cambridge and a doctorate in comparative law from the University of Edinburgh. In 1984, during a brief visit to Sudan, he was incarcerated for eighteen months by the Nimeiry regime for opposing the Second Sudanese Civil War and rejecting the adoption of *sharī'a* as state law. Given his lived experience of the political history in his native Sudan, it is unsurprising that An-Na'im presents an alternative to the Islamic state. His commitment to a liberalising approach to *sharī'a* can be seen as a direct response to the political and personal challenges he faced, and what he describes as a lifelong task of reconciling the values of tradition and modernity.[27]

---

[27] The basis of this biographical section stems from an interview with An-Na'im that I conducted at the Center for the Study of Law and Religion at Emory University (15 April 2023).

Islamic Ethics and the Reform of *Sharīʿa*

A core endeavour of An-Na'im's political thought is to redefine the concept of *sharīʿa* and examine the implications of this reinterpretation. This is a crucial task given his acknowledgement that *sharīʿa* plays a fundamental role in shaping and developing ethical norms and values for Muslims, retaining relevance whether Muslims are a majority or minority community (An-Na'im, 2008, p. 1). The term *sharīʿa*, An-Na'im argues, has two distinct dimensions. The first is a transcendental dimension that is unknowable. It comprises 'God's law in its divine and revealed sense' (An-Na'im, 2008, p. 264). The second dimension, historically developed through Islamic legal and juristic techniques (*usūl al-fiqh*), is formed through human interpretation and reasoning. It is this latter dimension which An-Na'im interrogates and seeks to reform on the grounds that *sharīʿa*, as positive law, is subject to human fallibility and error, and that its normative content is limited in scope and applicability (An-Na'im, 2008, p. 13). An-Na'im questions the origins, continuity, and authority of the Islamic jurisprudential tradition by abandoning its methods and techniques and nominally rehabilitating the principle of abrogation (*naskh*).[28] As such, he seeks to reinterpret *sharīʿa* by advancing two radical propositions for a modern Islamic ethics: an alternative hermeneutics of the Qur'an, and the replacement of traditional methods of Islamic positive law with a more 'dynamic and creative development' of Islamic law (An-Na'im, 2008, pp. 12–13). Both of these moves are controversial departures from the theological and juridical methods of Islamic moral argumentation.

The first of these propositions is directly influenced by the methodology of An-Na'im's intellectual and spiritual mentor, Ustadh Mahmoud Taha.[29] As An-Na'im explains: 'Taha proposed a revolutionary reform methodology, which he described as the evolution of Islamic legislation – in essence a call for the establishment of a new principle of interpretation that would permit applying some verses of Qur'an and accompanying Sunna instead of others' (An-Na'im, 1990, p. 34). Following Taha, An-Na'im advocates for a controversial

---

[28] Abrogation (*naskh*) refers to the phenomenon of a later verse of revelation altering a law or command established by a verse revealed earlier. The principle of *naskh* is accepted by the majority of Sunni Islamic jurists only insofar as its limited applicability to the early community of Muslims allows; these jurists approach it with great caution and scrutiny as it undermines the immutability of the Qur'an.

[29] A significant aspect of An-Nai'm's political thought is shaped by the intellectual and spiritual ideas of Ustadh Mahmoud Mahomed Taha (1909–85). As a law graduate in Khartoum in 1968, An-Na'im was drawn to Taha's socio-religious movement, the Republican Brotherhood (al-Ikhawaan al-jumhuriyyah), which was influenced by Sufi doctrine and liberal ideas. Taha's ideas and teachings as presented in *The Second Message of Islam* (1987) (later translated into English by An-Na'im) reinterpret the role of *sharīʿa* to address modern political and social challenges.

hermeneutical scheme that divides the message of the Qur'an into the Meccan and Medinan historical periods (Taha, 1987). Taha's rationale for this division is that early revelations of the Qur'an in Mecca represented the 'universal' and 'humane' message of Islam, while later ones in Medina were specific responses to the historical context of the early Islamic community (Taha, 1987, p. 161). For Taha, the earlier Meccan revelations of the Qur'an contain verses of peace (*ismah*) which emphasise freedom of choice, and these verses can be relied upon for constructing a new Islamic legal and ethical theory (Taha, 1987, pp. 125–126). While such a hermeneutical scheme accepts the totality of revelation, it employs the method of counter-abrogation (Taha, 1987, p. 31).[30] Taha's execution by the Islamic state of Sudan in 1985 on charges of apostasy signified that his 'death was the ultimate act in the advocacy of a liberal Islam, something he termed the second message of Islam' (An-Na'im, 1986, p. 206).[31]

In *Toward an Islamic Reformation*, An-Na'im's key legal text, he elaborates Taha's methodology to clarify its reformist aims:

> Is it possible for contemporary Muslims to reconsider the process of abrogation? Is it permissible to take verses that have been previously abrogated as the new basis of Islamic law and to that end deem previously enacted verses to be abrogated from the legal point of view? I submit that it is not only possible to rethink the rationale and consequences of *naskh* but that it is imperative to do so if we are to resolve the problems raised by the modern application of the public law of *shari'a*. (An-Na'im, 1990, p. 21)

For An-Na'im, the innovative and radical hermeneutics proposed by Taha could form a new intellectual foundation for a progressive, liberal conception of *sharī'a* compatible with human rights and modern democracy. An-Na'im acknowledges that Taha's re-interpretive approach may appear objectionable to many Muslims. However, he insists that his theory should not be viewed as an

---

[30] Abrogation (*naskh*) in the Qur'an refers to the phenomenon of a later verse of revelation altering a law or command established by a verse revealed earlier. In the *Second Message of Islam*, Taha outlines a method of counter-abrogation which suggests that the Meccan verses which come earlier must be treated as the foundation for Islamic law and later verses should be treated as marginal and of relevance only to the first Islamic political community.

[31] Howard (2001) recounts that between the 1960s and the 1980s, Taha was arrested multiple times for heresy. The denouncement of Taha's methodology as heresy by both the Islamic Al-Azhar University and the Muslim World League is historically documented (see O'Sullivan, 2003, p. 418). Taha was eventually executed by the Sudanese state on charges of apostasy in 1985. His writings continue to be banned in many parts of the Islamic world today. In the translator's introduction to the *Second Message of Islam*, An-Na'im states: '[t]he *Second Message of Islam* is particularly appealing to women, non-Muslims, and liberal educated Muslims in general. Despite the growing popularity of the republican ideology in the Sudan over the last decade, however, the core membership of the group still remains relatively small. Thousands of close sympathisers among the educated Muslim elites seem to be intimidated by the forces of established religious and political orthodoxy' (Taha, 1987, p. 27).

The Pluralistic Frameworks 43

external imposition or departure from Islam. Rather, it must be treated and evaluated as an internal reformation effort aimed at reformulating Islamic law from within the tradition itself: 'since the technique of *naskh* has been employed in the past to develop *shari'a* which has hitherto been accepted as the authentic and genuine Islamic model, the same technique may be employed today to produce an authentic and genuine modern Islamic law' (An-Na'im, 1990, p. 10). Recognising the ambitious and lifelong nature of the undertaking he has set for himself, An-Na'im remains steadfast in his pursuit of reformulating Islamic jurisprudence through innovative re-interpretive approaches. In his seminal work, *Islam and the Secular State*, he reaffirms his endorsement of Taha's methodology, citing his earlier works as a testament to its 'coherence' and 'viability' (An-Na'im, 2008, p. 124) in aligning Islam with liberal values.

An-Na'im's second proposition for a modern Islamic ethics is a reform of Islamic positive law. He argues that the fundamental structure and methodology of *sharī'a* has remained largely unchanged since the tenth century, with only limited practical adaptations in specific contexts (An-Na'im, 2008, p. 15). Although the tradition of Islamic jurisprudence likely served to stabilise Islamic societies in the early period of Islam, An-Na'im questions its durability and relevance for the contemporary context: he contends that the principle of consensus, which played a unifying role in bringing together the substantive content of Islamic legal schools, reduced the opportunity for creative thinking through *ijtihād*, the principle of independent juridical reasoning. An-Na'im criticises the limited scope assigned by Islamic jurists to independent reasoning, arguing that the 'closing of the gates *of ijtihād*' on the assumption that *sharī'a* had been exhaustively elaborated is a problematic approach to *sharī'a* since the tenth century (An-Na'im, 2008, p. 15).[32] Moreover, 'no human being institution should control this process' (An-Na'im, 2008, p. 14). While modern proponents of *sharī'a* often champion *ijtihad* and its accompanying juristic techniques for rethinking *sharī'a* in the contemporary context, An-Na'im surmises that is unlikely to engender sufficient reform, particularly in matters related to constitutional law, criminal justice, international law, and human rights. This is because many of the contentious rules in *sharī'a* stem directly from clear and unambiguous texts found in Islam's foundational sources of law, the Qur'an and *Sunnah* (An-Na'im, 1990, p. 49). There are tactical and political reasons for An-

---

[32] Hallaq regards this idea of the 'closure of the gate of *ijtihad*' as one of many inventions by legal orientalists such as Joseph Schacht (1964) to portray Islamic legal thought through a pernicious and degrading lens by emphasising its derivative nature and lack of originality (see Hallaq, 2002, pp. 28–29). Hallaq offers a comprehensive account of the origins of Islamic law and its subsequent formation which substantially challenges and calls into question the assertions and claims made by legal orientalists. Interestingly, An-Na'im (1990) draws liberally from Schacht's ideas to substantiate his arguments for legal reform.

Na'im's radical reform of the foundational aspects of *sharī'a* which become clearer when we evaluate his pluralistic framework.

Curiously, An-Na'im holds Ibn Rushd as an exemplary thinker from the Islamic intellectual tradition and draws explicitly on two of his ideas to strengthen his case for rethinking *sharī'a*.[33] First, An-Na'im cites Ibn Rushd to argue that the content of *sharī'a* evolves and changes over time as alternative methodologies come to be accepted and applied by Muslims: 'it should also be emphasised that *sharī'a* principles are always derived from human interpretation of the Qur'an and Sunna; they are what human beings can comprehend and seek to obey within their own specific historical context' (Ibn Rushd cited in An-Na'im, 2008, p. 10). Second, An-Na'im references Ibn Rushd's favoured method for Qur'anic hermeneutics which suggests that even when there is wide consensus on a particular meaning of the Qur'an among many generations, that meaning remains a claim about human understanding of the divine text. Consequently, Islamic consensus, An-Na'im argues, 'is what Ibn Rushd calls suppositional (*zanian*) and not certain' (An-Na'im, 2008, p. 47). An-Na'im contends that these arguments from Ibn Rushd highlight the inherent contradictions involved in identifying and ascribing legal normativity and by extension provide scope for radical reinterpretation of *sharī'a*. Presumably, An-Na'im turns to Ibn Rushd both for his veneration of reason and for finding juristic precedence for his argument on the evolution and reinterpretation of *sharī'a*. The question remains whether Ibn Rushd's statements are sufficient grounds for providing the kind of legal legitimacy An-Na'im requires for endorsing his radical project of Islamic legal reform. It is also altogether unlikely that Ibn Rushd would endorse a scheme of selective Qur'anic hermeneutics based on counter-abrogation. After all, as a rationalist thinker, Ibn Rushd emphasised internal coherence and lack of contradictions in understanding the Qur'an in its entirety and the act of selective abrogation of verses would greatly undermine this effort. Moreover, while extending the juridical scope for interpretation based on reason, Ibn Rushd largely operated within the mainstream Maliki jurisprudential tradition of his time. The notion of subjectively counter-abrogating verses would be an affront to the established juridical methods he operated within. Above all, however, Ibn Rushd remained wedded to the view that the Qur'an in its totality was a product of a miraculous event of divine revelation, 'that all matters are found in the Qur'an in the most complete way possible' and that the inviolability of the 'precious book' was a proof of the message of Islam (Ibn Rushd, 2001, p. 102).

---

[33] An-Na'im's invocation of Ibn Rushd's approach to *sharī'a* is typical of a broader impulse on the part of Islamic liberal thinkers seeking to excavate the origins of a liberalist, rationalist, or reformist strand of Islam from within the Islamic tradition (Rahman, 1982; Arkoun, 1994; Soroush, 1998). This is study that merits a more in-depth examination.

Modernity and the Mediation of Islamic Ethics and Politics

Modern Islamic political thought has been fundamentally shaped by its encounter with European modernity. European modernity has been conceived as both an intellectual project and a historical period. However, as Iqtidar (2011) and Bilgrami (2012) suggest, its broad use makes it difficult to analyse conceptually. This problem can be addressed without abandoning the term 'modernity' and by questioning its normative values and universalising logic. For many Islamic political thinkers, including An-Na'im, the *problem* of modernity is inseparable from the hegemony imposed on Islamic societies through colonialism and the advent of the nation state (An-Na'im, 2008, p. 31). The 1648 European Treaty of Westphalia not only formalised the indefeasible claims of political modernity but also reconfigured the relationship between politics and ethics through the notion of Lockean religious toleration.[34] While this may have settled centuries of war and conflict in Europe, paradoxically, it did not prevent the violent and anti-egalitarian conquest of indigenous people and lands, including those occupied by majority-Muslim societies. Islamic societies were rapidly transformed into modern polities devised along nationalistic lines, with a centralised form of authority and territorial sovereignty circumscribed by colonial borders that presupposed shared ethnic, religious, and political allegiance. An-Na'im argues that the territorial nation state defined citizenship in a contrived and coercive manner, disregarding the pre-existing historical and cultural formations in the Muslim world (An-Na'im, 2008, p. 33).

The rise of the nation state in the modern period presented key challenges for the Islamic world. On the one hand, it provided a prism for ordering politics and ethics across both East and West, by universally imposing a common institutional reality and a shared conceptual and normative framework (El Amine, 2016, p. 102). On the other hand (and this is one of the key features of European modernity), it sought to critically redefine and limit the role of religion. As such, the modern secular state now served to continuously 'manage the place of religious thought and action' (Iqtidar, 2011, pp. 64–65). At stake was the very nature of Islamic identity, the role of religion in public life, and the relationship between Islamic societies and the broader global community. The tradition of Islamic political theory has evolved eclectically in response to these developments. Various intellectual trends within modern Islamic political thought coalesced around the need to offer genuine 'Islamic solutions' to

---

[34] I use the term 'political modernity' to refer to the institutional aspects of the project of modernity that have sought to bureaucratise, centralise, and territorialise the state (El Amine, 2016, p. 106). As El Amine suggests, this political outcome is aligned with material processes, such as industrialisation and urbanisation, that produced a 'default form of political organization in Europe and whose normative and legal principles were later extended elsewhere' (El Amine, 2016, p. 106).

the challenges posed by Western colonialism and the resulting political and economic vulnerabilities experienced by Muslim societies (March, 2012, p. 11). As Muslim thinkers grappled with these issues, they navigated a complex landscape shaped by the legacy of colonialism, the demands of modernisation, and the desire to maintain authenticity and integrity in their religious traditions. The ongoing debates within modern Islamic political thought, exemplified by the contrasting approaches of An-Na'im and revivalist thinkers like Maududi and Qutb, reflect the urgency and significance of these challenges. An-Na'im contributes to these debates in a somewhat cautious manner. Islamic revivalist thinkers such as Maududi and Qutb, he suggests, are too concerned with creating a comprehensive alternative to modernity solely within an Islamic framework (An-Na'im, 2008, p. 273). By advancing limited and static conceptions of Islamic politics, their ideas are akin to the Soviet and fascist models of the totalitarian state which seeks to transform society in the image of the ruling party (An-Na'im, 2008, p. 292). The impetus to provide comprehensive solutions from within the Islamic tradition to modern problems, An-Na'im concedes, is a natural response of Muslims to social disorder, political powerlessness, and economic frustration (An-Na'im, 1990, p. 4). At its core, it represents the right to self-determination. However, this right must be balanced against the self-determination rights of others, especially in the public sphere where competing claims in Islamic pluralistic societies require 'mediation and accommodation' (An-Na'im, 1990, p. 4). One way this may be achieved is by reconciling Muslim commitment to *sharī'a* with a form of secularism that coheres within a religious framework (An-Na'im, 1990, p. 10). While this is the guiding premise of An-Na'im's pluralistic framework, a key aspect of its practical realisation is contingent on the radical reform of *sharī'a* as I have illustrated. As An-Na'im affirms, 'demonstrating that the public law aspects of *sharī'a* developed by founding jurists are not truly divine would enable their replacement without violating Muslim religious sensibilities' (An-Na'im, 1990, p. 10). This statement brings into sharp relief the ethico-political problem An-Na'im sets up for himself. Does a radical reform of *sharī'a* achieve the intended reconciliation with secularism that An-Na'im desires, or does it produce the opposite effect – alienating large segments of the Muslim public?

Islam and the 'Secular'

An-Na'im's defence for a secular state in Islam argues that it holds greater promise for promoting Islamic ethical values such as 'social justice, peace, goodness, and virtue' than any Islamic state which implements *sharī'a* as state law (An-Na'im, 2008, p. 293). Yet to truly grasp the significance of this defence, I argue, one must first examine the concept of the secular itself. The secular, unassailable to the logic of the modern state, is a concept that not only serves to separate religion from politics (or church from state) but also assumes that its own ideas and values are universally applicable and normatively superior, regardless of their context-specific origins and limitations. Talal Asad's (2003) ground-breaking *Formations of the Secular* clarifies why the term 'secular' should also be thought of as conceptually prior to the political doctrine of secularism. Asad suggests that the term 'secular' evolved over time 'through a variety of concepts, practices, and sensibilities' (Asad, 2003, p. 16). As a temporal and spatial concept, the term 'secular' functioned to establish, authorise, and perpetuate distinctively modern and European modes of being and knowing, revealing its inherent normative power. In a secular purview, religion, as a domain of faith and passion, was considered to be at loggerheads with politics, the domain of rational argument and interest-guided action. As such, religion, rooted in divine authority and constraint, was viewed as a threat to individual freedom and the freedom of others (Asad, 1999, p. 182). The place of religion in modern life therefore needed to be revised: 'in order for a society to be modern, it has to be secular, and for it to be secular, it has to relegate religion to non-political spaces' (Asad, 1999, p. 179). Asad's critique encapsulates the limitations of the concept of the secular for Islamic normative inquiry. By retaining a normative power in defining and delimiting what is considered religious or non-religious, the term 'secular' lacks conceptual impartiality.

The doctrine of secularism should not be thought of as a neutral framework but a form of power that inflects political institutions and ideas such as liberalism, human rights, and the modern state. As Iqtidar points out, secularism can be better understood as a political project imbricated in the complex interplay of history and politics, distinct from the European historical process of secularisation and theories of secularisation (Iqtidar, 2011, p. 20). Secularism, constituted as it is by liberal ideas, possesses a normative and universalist currency that is often asserted polemically against Islam, such that the latter is perceived as inimical to progress (Gellner, 1991; Huntington, 1993; Lewis, 2002). The tension that modern Islamic political thinkers thus seek to resolve is how to reconcile liberal democracy sustained by secularism with the theological resources at their disposal (Hashemi, 2009, p. 1). Hashemi suggests that one way of confronting this paradox is to interrogate the form of secularism that has been integrated into the political culture of Muslim societies (Hashemi, 2009, p. 2). In societies where religion plays a significant role in identity, one path to reconciling secularism with religion might involve the development of a theory of secularism rooted in religious perspectives (Hashemi, 2009, p. 2). To accomplish this, Islamic thinkers must formulate a theory of secularism that harmonises with both the essential operational prerequisites of liberal democracy and their own political and theological perspectives.

An-Na'im's theory of a secular state in Islam might count as one such effort.[35] It takes as its starting point a distinct theological position on the radical reform of *sharī'a*. From here, it proceeds to advance a case for the secular in Islam, despite the conceptual complexities of its linguistic appropriation. As Piscatori and Eickelman (1996, p. 39) suggest, the idea of the secular is commonly viewed by Muslims as a foreign concept antagonistic to religion. For the most part, An-Na'im acknowledges the complexity of such a theoretical endeavour. Muslims, he suggests, tend to be hostile to the concept of secularism because of the polemical nature of its use and the rigidity of some of its theoretical definitions (An-Na'im, 2008, p. 36). To overcome this, An-Na'im suggests that secularism must be thought of as a fluid and variegated concept that can be usefully appropriated rather than rejected. This is because secularism does not constitute the exclusion of religion from the public life of any society. Those who define it in this limiting way are chasing an 'illusory notion' that is not even valid for liberal societies where secularism is rooted (An-Na'im, 2008, p. 36). Curiously, An-Na'im abandons the term 'secularism' on the grounds that it conflates the state and politics, opting instead for the term 'secular state'. This has obvious definitional implications which he proceeds to qualify. A secular state in Islam is an institutional form where there is neutrality regarding religious doctrine and the freedom of individuals within the state are safeguarded through the mechanisms of human rights, constitutionalism, and citizenship (An-Na'im, 2008, p. 24). This separation of Islam from the state does not mean the relegation of Islam to the private domain and its exclusion from Muslim public life (An-Na'im, 2008, pp. 8–9). Islam can continue to interact productively with politics, and religious values can positively influence political debate: 'allowing *sharī'a* principles to play a positive role in public life without permitting them to be implemented through state institutions ... is a delicate balance that each society must strive to maintain for itself over time' (An-Na'im, 2008, p. 38).

The idea of completely separating Islam from politics is deemed unnecessary or even undesirable. Muslims, An-Na'im contends, naturally integrate their religious beliefs into their political actions (An-Na'im, 2008, p. 4). Such an

---

[35] In his book *Islam and the Principles of Governance* (*al-Islam wa-Usul al-Hukm*), the Egyptian scholar Ali-Abdel Razeq called for Muslims to differentiate between religion and government as spheres with distinct purposes (see Razeq, 2012). He argued that Islamic law and ethics encompassed conduct, manners, and customs that were entirely separate from methods of political rule and civil government. Moreover, he theorised that the idea of an Islamic caliphate was a human innovation rather than a religious imperative. An-Na'im acknowledges the significance of Al-Razeq's thesis for his own political project, which seeks to establish the validity of a secular state within an Islamic context (An-Na'im, 2008, p. 1). However, An-Na'im takes Al-Razeq's ideas in a new direction by developing a framework that is interpretative rather than theological.

assertion sheds light on the paradoxical nature of a secular approach which seeks to actively delimit the operationalisation of Islam in the political sphere whilst conceding that Muslims infuse their political aspirations with their deeply held religious beliefs. It would therefore benefit readers if An-Na'im provided further insight into why he believes this separation is neither necessary nor desirable. Could *sharī'a*, according to his perspective, yield positive outcomes for Islamic politics? If so, what might these outcomes entail, and which aspects of the religious principles of *sharī'a* would meaningfully cohere with the liberal instruments of human rights and constitutionalism that he sets up as institutional safeguards? A resolution to this question appears to depend on his crucial formulation for a radical methodology for the reform of *sharī'a*. Taha provides An-Na'im with a juristic foundation for constructing a modern Islamic public law: 'whether this particular methodology is accepted or rejected by contemporary Muslims, the need for drastic reform of the public law of *sharī'a*', is for An-Na'im, 'beyond dispute' (An-Na'im, 1990, p. 186). In An-Na'im's definition of the secular state in Islam, we can also identify the complex interplay of mediating Islamic ethics and politics. By suggesting a drastic reform of *sharī'a* and by implementing human rights and constitutional safeguards, An-Na'im is making an important move vis-à-vis *sharī'a*: diminishing its existing status and calling for its regulation under liberal political instruments. Critics may perceive this attempt to liberalise *sharī'a* by challenging its epistemic foundations as reinforcing the universalising pretensions of secular and liberal values and asserting their superiority. Arguably, a serious engagement with the endogenous modes within the Islamic tradition to achieve a form of reconciliation that exemplifies Islam's commitment to the values of plurality and tolerance is likely to have prevented such a critique.[36]

Institutional Forms: Islam and 'the State'

An-Na'im's normative proposal of a secular state in Islam is predicated on the acceptance of the modern sovereign state as the unit of analysis. While conceding that this European model of state formation is a colonial imposition on Muslim lands, An-Na'im views the ubiquity and universalisation of the state in the international order in realist terms. Any attempt to articulate norms for Islamic societies must take into account the drastic transformation brought about by the modern state and its impact on premodern state formations (An-Na'im, 2008, p. 285). An Islamic prototype for governance cannot be excavated

---

[36] A contemporary example of this approach is evident in the work of Rached Ghannouchi, who proposes that the Universal Declaration of Human Rights, can be widely accepted by Muslims under the correct interpretation of Islamic law and theology. See *Public Freedoms in the Islamic State* (Ghannouchi, 2022).

from the life of Prophet Muhammad (An-Na'im, 2008, p. 53). That was a model that is impossible to re-enact because no other human being can claim the Prophet Muhammad's combination of religious and political authority: '[a]s the ultimate embodiment of this model, the Prophet was accepted by Muslims to be their sole legislator, judge, and commander. That experience was unique and cannot be replicated because Muslims do not accept the possibility of prophets after the Prophet Muhammad' (An-Na'im, 2008, p. 53). This determination that an Islamic prototype for governance cannot be excavated from the Prophetic example grants An-Na'im latitude to revisit the question of political legitimacy in Islam. Specifically, it allows him to deny the possibility of merging religious and political functions within a single authority, an idea that aligns with his broader argument advocating for an Islamic secular state.

An-Nai'm observes that two types of Islamic governance can be extrapolated from Islamic history: one of conflation and the other of convergence (An-Na'im, 2008, p. 53). Conflation exists when there is no separation between state and religious institutions, while convergence marks the complete separation between religious and political authorities. Contemporary Muslim rulers tend to implicitly combine religious and political roles, even if they do not explicitly admit to doing so, likely due to the importance of appearing Islamically legitimate in the eyes of their populace (An-Na'im, 2008, p. 53). The point of identifying this distinction is to prompt Muslims to accept the impossibility of the conflation and convergence models, and to redirect their attention to the possibility of a secular state in Islam. Such a state accedes to territorial sovereignty and other normative apparatus of the European model as a pragmatic and historical reality: 'Islamic societies choose to be bound by a minimum set of national and international obligations of membership in the world community of territorial states"(An-Na'im, 2008, p. 19). These changes cannot simply be reversed as the state is a firmly embedded sociopolitical reality. Muslims now live within territorial nation states characterised by a centralised and bureaucratically organised administrative and legal order (An-Na'im, 2008, p. 19). Citing Weber, he clarifies that the purpose of the state is to exert authority over what occurs within its area of territorial jurisdiction through a monopoly of the use of legitimate force (An-Na'im, 2008, p. 285).

A secular state in Islam rests on both the ineluctability of the modern state system and the impossibility of reviving precolonial modes of Islamic governance. This is a clear endorsement of political realism, sharply at variance with those approaches that seek to reinstate a modern caliphate unconstrained by colonial borders. The emphasis on the viability of the modern state for Muslims is most prominently critiqued by the thinker Wael Hallaq (2013). Hallaq argues that the modern state is a highly problematic institutional arrangement for all societies but poses an additional problem for Muslims: the harm it can do to *sharīʿa* when *sharīʿa* is imposed through the state. Hallaq takes for granted the long tradition of reform within *sharīʿa* and suggests that the modern state is an inferior model to premodern forms of Islamic governance (Hallaq, 2013, p. 5). The adoption of the modern state by Muslims, Hallaq contends, generates an impossible and self-contradictory task for reconciling ethics and politics in Islam, which Islam has never regarded as separate domains. This is because the state is not politically neutral but dominates the process of subjectivity formation through universalising ideals and a paradigm of ethics often hostile to Islam (Hallaq, 2013, p. 75).[37] For Hallaq, Islamic ethical values, in contrast, are grounded on noumenal reason with an entirely different consciousness of self and entirely different interpretation of man. Premodern Muslims, Hallaq surmises, viewed *sharīʿa* as an ethical system with a lived tradition of moral values that permeated social and political life.

While both An-Na'im and Hallaq reject the possibility of the modern state enforcing *sharīʿa*, their rationales and prescriptions for mediating the tension between Islamic ethics and politics differ significantly. There are two major points of disagreement between them regarding the nature of this rejection. First, Hallaq argues that any conception of a modern Islamic state is 'inherently self-contradictory' because *sharīʿa*, by definition, constitutes the informal rulings of jurists based on a commitment to God's legislative sovereignty, whereas the modern state requires top-down codification of law premised on the state's own sovereign authority (Hallaq, 2013, ix). Thus, for Hallaq, the authority of *sharīʿa* cannot be re-enacted through the institutional apparatus of the modern state. An-Na'im's rejection of *sharīʿa* codification by the modern state differs in its emphasis on the nature and interpretation of *sharīʿa* itself. He contends that *sharīʿa* cannot be conclusively and infallibly interpreted, especially by Islamic jurists, and those states seeking to apply *sharīʿa* as law enforce tyranny (An-Na'im, 2008, p. 28). The second disagreement concerns mediating Islamic ethics and modern politics. Hallaq posits that Islamic ethics, embedded in *sharīʿa*, exhibits flexibility, adaptability, and internal pluralism – resources capable of nourishing a modern Islamic politics. Conversely, An-Na'im argues that while some Islamic ethical principles and social values are necessary for Islamic societies' proper functioning, *sharīʿa* requires reformation to cohere with liberal values such as equality, freedom, human rights, and democracy.

---

[37] For example, modern states privilege the Enlightenment concept of autonomous rationality, epitomised by Kant's account of pure practical reason, which is sharply at odds with Islamic normative ethics derived from divine law (Hallaq, 2013, p. 75). Similarly, Hobbes' influential account of the state reifies the notion of morality as objectively discovered by human reason, rather than seeing morality as based on tradition or scriptural authority (Hallaq, 2013, p. 79).

There is also a profound difference between An-Na'im and Hallaq in terms of identifying what needs greater reform: the state or *sharī'a*. An-Na'im takes the state as a given and seeks to reform *sharī'a*, while Hallaq takes *sharī'a* as a given and seeks to reform the state. It is open to debate which is the more 'realistic' or pragmatic position. At its core, An-Na'im's mediation of Islamic ethics and politics by reforming *sharī'a* forms part of a broader intellectual project to reconcile *sharī'a* with the extra-Islamic tradition of liberal thought, the specifics of which we can observe in his pluralistic framework.

Reconciling *Sharī'a* and Liberal Thought

An-Na'im notes the guiding principles of his pluralistic framework as follows: a repudiation of dichotomies between so-called Western and Islamic concepts and institutions, and a consideration of the relevance and utility of extra-Islamic traditions of thought, 'regardless of their origin' (An-Na'im, 2008, p. 97).[38] These principles reveal the contours of An-Na'im's pluralistic approach which strives to collapse artificial binaries between the 'West' and Islam and to synthesise and incorporate diverse traditions towards accommodation rather than conflict. Such an argument posits that it is misleading to view the 'West' or the 'Muslim world' as monolithic entities, as historical interactions between early Islamic scholars and diverse traditions of thought proved intellectually generative in the past (An-Na'im, 2008, p. 98). Such cross-pollination of ideas must continue into the present for Islamic thought to remain dynamic and pluralistic. Moreover, due to cultural and intellectual hegemony, Muslim readers likely have a greater sense of 'familiarity' and 'appreciation' of 'Western' intellectual ideas as opposed to their own traditions of thought (An-Na'im, 2008, p. 98). In this spirit of unquestioning pragmatism, An-Na'im sets forth to engage with the ideas of John Rawls, albeit with a caveat. To explore liberal political thought without being bound or limited by it, and with a recognition of the risks of transplanting its premises and theoretical assumptions onto Islamic societies (An-Na'im, 2008, p. 100).

There is no doubt that the ideas of John Rawls, the influential twentieth-century American liberal philosopher, have sparked extensive debate within contemporary political theory. These debates have inflected Islamic political thinking, initiating important debates that scrutinise the compatibility of Rawlsian liberal principles with Islamic teachings (Haider, 2006; Fadel, 2008; Khan, 2017; March, 2011). An-Na'im's political thought can be analysed as part of this tradition of pluralistic engagement with Rawls, marked by what he terms as a 'friendly amendment' to Rawls' account of political liberalism (An-Na'im,

---

[38] The category of Western, while problematic for its historical anachronism, forms part of An-Na'im's conceptual vocabulary.

2014, p. 242). This 'friendly amendment' involves a re-evaluation of Rawls' concept of public reason, with the objective of reconciling its key features within an Islamic framework. The starting point of his engagement is to reconsider Rawls' contention that in a just and stable democratic society, public reason is neutral with respect to religion. Public reason as Rawls defined it comprised 'the reason of equal citizens who, as a collective body, exercise final political and coercive power over one another in enacting laws and in amending the constitution' (Rawls, 1993b, p. 223). In liberal societies, public reason therefore operates as political value which citizens who seek or hold public office employ to justify their political decisions through a set of publicly endorsed values and standards (Rawls, 1993b, pp. 213–216). Public reason as a core feature of Rawls' liberal thought underlines the principle of reciprocity, the notion that political power is used in ways that all citizens may reasonably be expected to endorse. The content of public reason is formulated through a 'political conception of justice' that specifies key liberal principles which include 'basic rights, liberties, and opportunities' (Rawls, 1993b, p. 223).

Rawls maintains that a central feature of liberal democracy is the presence of 'reasonable pluralism', marked by conflicting comprehensive doctrines, including religious belief (Rawls, 1993b, p. 765). One way to establish a common ground, or an 'overlapping consensus' where citizens can agree on a shared set of principles for the basic structure of society, is public reason. The doctrine of public reason holds that 'comprehensive doctrines of truth or right be replaced by an idea of the politically reasonable addressed to citizens as citizens' (Rawls, 1993b, p. 766). Public reason for Rawls must be insulated from the comprehensive religious, philosophical, and moral doctrines that these citizens may hold as true in other contexts. The reason for this is simple; if public reason were to incorporate specific religious doctrines, it could exclude some citizens whose beliefs do not align with those doctrines.[39]

For An-Na'im, Rawls' theory of public reason does not accommodate Islamic societies, where *sharī'a* is central to ethical and political life (An-Na'im, 2014, p. 245). An-Na'im critiques two main claims about religion and politics that Rawls advances: first, that religious reasons are not appropriate in public political discourse because they are not accessible to all citizens and

---

[39] Rawls argues, 'central to the idea of public reason is that it neither criticises nor attacks any comprehensive doctrine, religious or nonreligious, except insofar as that doctrine is incompatible with the essentials of public reason and a democratic polity. The basic requirement is that a reasonable doctrine accepts a constitutional democratic regime and its companion idea of legitimate law' (Rawls, 1993b, p. 766). In addition, any comprehensive religious view 'should give way in public life' (Rawls, 1993a, p. 10). As such, no comprehensive religious view features either negatively within public reason, as the target of criticism, or positively within public reason, as a supporting basis of political argument.

cannot be subject to public scrutiny and debate; and second, that it is not possible for citizens to affirm a religious doctrine and hold a reasonable political conception that supports a just democratic regime. Both of these are objectionable, according to An-Na'im, as they impose a 'stipulation of what qualifies as "public" reason in one setting or another' (An-Na'im, 2014, p. 245). In other words, while it is important for citizens to have a shared conception of political authority, this shared understanding should not be limited or defined by a set of principles: 'If the reasons that citizens advance and their manner of reasoning actively undermine a shared conception of political authority, then that is a separate inquiry to pursue, without insisting on a blanket rejection of one type of reason or another' (An-Na'im, 2014, p. 245). This determination does not constitute a dismissal of Rawls, but an amendment of his theory.

To further articulate his critique of Rawls' limited conception of public reason in relation to comprehensive doctrines, An-Na'im draws on another thinker from the tradition of liberal thought, Jurgen Habermas. Habermas' (1995) critique of Rawls' distinction between comprehensive doctrines and political values, as well as the division of public and private life, provides An-Na'im with the intellectual resources to further solidify his argument. As Habermas outlines, Rawls' conception of comprehensive doctrines fails to recognise the historically fluid boundaries between the public and private realms and the significance of independent and non-governmental spaces as essential areas for the expression and development of public reason (An-Na'im, 2008, p. 100).[40] Building on Habermas' critique, An-Na'im attempts to formulate a conception of public reason within an Islamic framework, something he terms 'civic reason'. Civic reason is a political structure that mediates public policy and legislation through reasoning that citizens can accept or reject. It promotes public debate and deliberation to develop a common set of shared values and ethical principles (An-Na'im, 2014, p. 257). The word 'civic' is deliberately used by An-Na'im to invoke the need for policy and legislation to be accepted by the public at large, and for fora of rational debate to remain open and accessible to all citizens (An-Na'im, 2008, p. 7). This conception of civic reason seeks to balance the individual's right to freedom of religion and the collective pursuit of justice by recognising that religious beliefs can contribute

---

[40] Habermas (1995) distinguishes between the public sphere, which is the broad political space where public discourse takes place, and public reason, which represents the norms and principles that shape the quality and fairness of public discourse. Unlike Habermas, who emphasises the critical-rational dimension of the public sphere as enmeshed in power relations (Asad, 1999, p. 180; Iqtidar, 2011, p. 18), An-Na'im offers a relatively uncomplicated view of the public sphere as a space for the cultivation of Islamic norms and ethics, expressed in formal and informal learning, institutions of worship, and the delivery of social services (An-Na'im, 2008, p. 80).

The Pluralistic Frameworks

to public discussion and decision-making in politics. Unlike Rawls' concept of public reason, which relies on impartial reasoning, civic reason accommodates for religious beliefs to shape the discourse of public policy and law. In this sense, civic reason aims to negotiate the centrality of *sharī'a* by providing a mechanism for its deliberation in the context of a secular state (An-Na'im, 2014, p. 257). Civic reason allows aspects of *sharī'a* to reflect public law and policy insofar as it adheres to constitutional and human rights safeguards (An-Na'im, 2014, p. 247).

An-Na'im's pluralistic framework enables the normative rethinking of Islamic politics through civic reason. By repurposing Rawls' conception of public reason and presenting it through a new register of civic reason, An-Na'im suggests that Islamic societies can achieve a Rawlsian form of overlapping consensus. The basic problem with Rawls' approach is that it does not consider societies outside of the Anglo-American experience, including Islamic societies where religious identity and values extensively shape the public sphere. The *sharī'a* is an integral part of the common understanding of Muslims and its precepts extend beyond merely religious rituals and jurisprudence (An-Na'im, 2014, p. 246).

In the context of An-Na'im's theory of a secular state in Islam, civic reason can be operationalised by creating a space for public discourse that is open to diverse perspectives of *sharī'a*. This approach can help to defuse the tensions that arise from separating Islam from the state while recognising its place in the Muslim public. Islamic principles and ethical norms can, for example, be proposed for adoption by these states as official public policy or legislation through the process of civic reason but without reference to specific religious laws. Since forms of civic reason are already present to some degree in most Islamic societies, An-Na'im calls for their 'further conscious and incremental development' in the Islamic postcolonial world (An-Na'im, 2008, p. 8). Implementing civic reason in Islamic societies is a complex and ongoing process that would require ongoing dialogue and negotiation and can be regarded as an idea that is 'tentative and evolving' (An-Na'im, 2008, p. 101). Crucially, civic reason should vary according to Islamic local histories and conditions because the principles of human rights and democracy ought to be understood and applied within specific cultural, historical, and social contexts (An-Na'im 2008, p. 101).

An-Na'im is correct in arguing that *sharī'a* even in its present iteration cannot be excised from Islamic public life. In the contemporary world its influence extends even into liberal secular democracies, where it continues to shape Muslim attitudes and discourses around ethics and morality. If observed voluntarily, *sharī'a* is more likely to play a significant role in shaping and developing ethical norms and values that can ultimately be reflected in legislation and public policy through the democratic political process. To address concerns around codifying religious norms in a secular state, An-Na'im could delineate between prescriptive/proscriptive norms and permissive norms with a religious content An-Na'im's argument may be enhanced by delineating between prescriptive or proscriptive norms and permissive norms. Secular liberals may endorse permissive norms with a religious content, such as allowing religious ceremonies for marriage or attending religious educational institutions. However, they may worry about prescriptive or proscriptive norms with a religious content, such as mandatory attendance at religious educational institutions. Further clarification from An-Na'im on the specific kinds of 'official policy and legislation' he envisions enacting Islamic religious values, and whether these include prescriptive or proscriptive norms, could enhance his argument. Additionally, it would be beneficial to understand what differentiates An-Na'im's legislative and policy proposals from those of liberal multiculturalism (see, for example, Kymlicka, 1995). To distinguish his approach, An-Na'im could further elaborate on how his *sharī'a* reforms notions of civic reason that diverge from or expand upon Kymlicka's prescriptions for accommodating cultural pluralism through differentiated citizenship rights.

The Plausibility of An-Na'im's Pluralistic Framework

In his paper 'The Idea of Public Reason Revisited', Rawls (1997) discusses the challenges of accommodating reasonable pluralism and acknowledges the limits to which some comprehensive doctrines can be accommodated within a liberal democratic framework., Rawls cites An-Na'im's writings on Islamic constitutionalism as a perfect example of an overlapping consensus (Rawls, 1997, pp. 782–783). Rawls argues that An-Na'im's reinterpretation of *sharī'a* is far more consistent with the constraints of public reason and essential constitutional liberties, providing a way for Muslims to reconcile their religious and political commitments in a liberal democratic framework (Rawls, 1997, p. 782).[41] Curiously, Rawls makes two important remarks related to Islamic ethics. First, he notes that An-Na'im presents his interpretation of *sharī'a* as 'correct and superior' to gain acceptability amongst Muslims. Second, Rawls observes that An-Na'im's main arguments for radical reform of *sharī'a* flow

---

[41] An-Na'im's reconciliation of liberal thought and *sharī'a* encompasses various legal reforms aimed at harmonising religious and political commitments within a liberal democratic framework. While Rawls doesn't provide specific examples, An-Na'im furnishes detailed explanations of the political implications of his legal reforms in relation to modern constitutionalism, criminal justice, modern international law, and human rights (see chapters 4–7, *Towards an Islamic Reformation*, 1996).

from the teachings of Taha, which reject the traditional understanding of *sharī'a* (Rawls, 1997, p. 783). Rawls' observation here is significant insofar as its implicit suggestion that the sophistication of An-Na'im's political theory is enabled by a particular reformist vision. An-Na'im's adoption of Taha's method that includes profane and arguably heretical elements enables, from Rawls' vantage point, its success in reconciling political liberalism and Islam through an overlapping consensus. The question then remains, does the possibility of reconciling Islam and liberal thought through an 'overlapping consensus' rely on radical proposals for metaphysical and hermeneutical innovation of *sharī'a*?

In conclusion, An-Na'im's pluralistic framework represents a bold attempt to mediate Islamic ethics and politics by incorporating the extra-Islamic tradition of liberal thought and reconciling its ideas with *sharī'a*. However, as I have outlined in this section, this mediation of Islamic ethics and politics radically departs from authentic or traditional understandings of *sharī'a*. Such a departure is exemplified in the subversion of *sharī'a* under liberal instruments by recommending the radical reform of Islamic legal normativity, principally through the theological innovation of the method of counter-abrogation. While An-Na'im seeks to make a case for the interdependency of ethics and politics in Islam, he does so from premises that are unlikely to be acceptable to the vast majority of devout Muslims. What is lacking from An-Na'im's pluralistic framework, I argue, is the 'principle of plausibility', described by March as follows:

> The crucial features of such an affirmation are that it be both acceptable from a liberal standpoint ... and sufficiently Islamic to be plausible to believers (i.e., to help solve the basic problem of the rejectionist doctrine) ... Asking what Islamic doctrine would have to affirm for it to be said that it is providing believers with both authentic and principled reasons for endorsing [it] is best perceived as the search for a certain kind of equilibrium, namely, for that fully reasonable account of the minimal demands [that are] least in conflict with the aims and spirit of Islamic political ethics. (March, 2011, p. 96)

The principle of plausibility posits that any framework devised for the ethical and political reform of Islamic society should aim to mitigate conflict with prevailing Islamic doctrinal beliefs, as embraced by its adherents. March's study *Islam and Liberal Citizenship* (2011) demonstrates the efficacy of this principle by exploring the potential for an overlapping consensus between Islamic ethics and political liberalism. March argues that Islam, as a reasonable comprehensive doctrine, contains sufficient moral and legal resources for accepting the demands of liberal citizenship. This insight is important because it highlights the need for 'pluralistic frameworks' that seek to mediate Islamic ethics and politics by incorporating extra-Islamic traditions of thought in a way that recognises the central moral questions of the Islamic tradition. This principle serves as a crucial guideline for evaluating the success and potential impact of such frameworks. A successful pluralistic framework must find an equilibrium that minimises conflict with the score beliefs and principles of the Islamic tradition while still achieving a meaningful synthesis or dialogue between them. Finally, it underscores the importance of considering the reception and acceptance of pluralistic frameworks within the communities they seek to address. A framework that departs too radically from the established beliefs and practices of a community may struggle to gain traction, even if it is intellectually innovative or compelling from an outsider's perspective. To be effective, Islamic pluralistic frameworks must be sensitive to the lived experiences, moral intuitions, and religious commitments of the Islamic audience it seeks to engage.

Finally, it is reasonable suggest that An-Na'im does not fully succeed in circumventing the *theo-political* problem he sets out to resolve. It remains to be seen whether An-Na'im's normative proposal for a secular state in Islam can be persuasive within majority-Muslim societies, given its entanglement with a highly unorthodox, revisionist approach to Islamic law and ethics.[42] To answer this question, one must ask to what extent An-Na'im's conception of Islamic ethics directly informs his normative theory of politics. While An-Na'im gestures at the possibilities of utilising other methodological approaches to reform, it is highly unlikely that such possibilities might look to the internal resources of *sharī'a* in the traditional sense, given An-Na'im's excoriating critique of the tradition of Islamic legal normativity. This is unfortunate, considering the breadth of *sharī'a*, which possesses a formidable capaciousness for accommodating a range of positions. Ultimately, a radical break from the Islamic ethical tradition runs the risk of appearing as a marginal contribution to the Islamic political tradition. Despite An-Na'im's creativity, sophistication, and originality in developing a pluralistic framework, this claim rings true.

4 Rethinking Islamic Politics: Pluralistic Frameworks and the Future

By way of conclusion, I shall consider how the foregoing comparative inquiry of the pluralistic frameworks of Ibn Rushd and An-Na'im can offer some useful insights for rethinking the future of Islamic politics. These insights are premised on four ideas about Islamic ethics outlined in the introduction. First, Islam is

---

[42] In his later writings, An-Na'im is more attentive to the central ethical dilemma of plausibility. He admits, more plainly, the theological currency of *sharī'a* as traditionally understood, suggesting that an overwhelming majority of Muslims prefer to conform to an understanding of *sharī'a* as practised in their local communities rather than exercise individual choice (An-Na'im, 2014, p. 246). This leads An-Na'im to a more forthright criticism of Rawls: 'Muslims maintain the right and duty to seek *sharī'a* justification,' and such a right is crucial to their right of religious self-determination (An-Na'im, 2014, p. 246).

The Pluralistic Frameworks 59

a religious tradition based on law and ethics, and its normative system, *sharī'a*, contains a divine, sacred, and transcendental component derived from revelation. Second, *sharī'a* is not embodied in a single authoritative code and cannot be regarded as a monolithic and static category. Rather, it is evolving and dynamic drawing on methods and techniques which rely on probability and reason. Third, the foundational texts of Islam, the Qur'an and Hadith, which underpin *sharī'a* are the basis of the Islamic 'discursive tradition' which defines and determine the boundaries of an Islamic universal orthodoxy (Anjum, 2007). The relative stability of this boundary distinguishes Islam from other ethical and moral traditions which relinquish any notion of foundationalism. Fourth, apart from legal norms *sharī'a* functions as an indispensable ethical imaginary for Muslim self-identification and self-understanding. All these ideas encapsulate the centrality of *sharī'a* and its varied manifestations and help us to determine what is at stake in separating ethics and politics in Islam.

To begin, one striking feature of the pluralistic frameworks of Ibn Rushd and An-Na'im is their critical and unorthodox engagement with the methods of the Islamic tradition.[43] However, the form of this methodological engagement is hardly similar, revealing their vastly different contextual environments, unique fidelities, and preferences to religious and political ideas. In the context of twelfth-century Muslim Spain, theological debates had enormous political implications due to the intertwined nature of religion and governance. The Almohad imperial order had ushered in a distinct theological orientation towards Ash'arī kalam, replacing the austere and literalist outlook of their Almoravid predecessors. Throughout his writings, Ibn Rushd displays an abiding interest in identifying and disabusing 'deviant' theological strands that had gained political currency:

> On this issue, people in [this] religion have been greatly confused, to the point of splintering into many erring groups and different sects, each group believing that it is following the original religion and branding whoever disagrees with it as either a heretic or an unbeliever (*Kāfir*) whose blood and property are free for all. All this is a departure from the intent of the lawgiver, occasioned by their mistaken understanding of the intent of religion. (Ibn Rushd, 2001, p. 17)

In the treatise *Exposition of Religious Argument*, Ibn Rushd presents an exhaustive critique competing theological schools (Ash'arites, Mu'tazalites, literalists,

---

[43] Here, we may refer to orthodoxy in a different sense to its universal counterpart. Local or informal orthodoxy in Islamic intellectual history constituted the debates and informal opinions of scholars which gained 'public recognition' (Jackson, 2002, p. 30). This form of orthodoxy often converged with structures of power and was fundamentally concerned with regulating the acceptable boundaries for discussing matters of doctrine and belief.

esoterics) by examining the flaws in their methodological approaches: 'if all such beliefs were examined and compared with the intent of religion, it would appear that most of them are novel statements and heretical interpretations' (Ibn Rushd, 2001, p. 17). Presumably, his most thoroughgoing critique of *kalām*, directed at the ideas of al-Ghazali in particular, was due to its rising political popularity.[44] Some scholars have rightly submitted that Ibn Rushd intended to criticise *kalām*, insofar as he perceived it as a theological orthodoxy that needed to be replaced (Hourani, 1985; Leaman, 1988).[45] Rather than relying on the 'problematic dialectic, scripture-based epistemology, and occasionalism of kalam theology', Ibn Rushd showcased philosophy, grounded in empirical demonstration, as an alternate intellectual basis for shaping political and intellectual life in Almohad society. (Adamson & Di Giovanni, 2018, p. 7). This suggests that Ibn Rushd was not content to simply opine on religious debates, but strategically positioned himself and his ideas in relation to the power dynamics between the rulers and religious scholars (*ulama*) of Almohad society. Crucially, Ibn Rushd's task here was to clearly articulate the content of a new, authentic, Islamic philosophical orthodoxy.

In his legal scholarship, however, the tenor of his writings is somewhat different. *The Distinguished Jurists Primer*, his major legal compendium, comprises familiar juridical techniques of Maliki *fiqh* that help to shape the Almohad public discourse on *sharī'a* and Islamic legal normativity. The primary purpose of this legal manual, Ibn Rushd argued, was to train individuals aspiring to practise *ijtihād* to enable them to pass independent judgment on novel cases instead of relying on past rulings (Ibn Rushd, 2000, p. 4). But Ibn Rushd's legal epistemology is also infused with the methods of Aristotelian philosophy, particularly from his works on logic and *Rhetoric*. Here, some have made the case that Ibn Rushd develops something akin to a 'philosophy of law' which harmonises Islamic juristic methods and Aristotelian rhetoric principally through the notion of probability (Bouhafa, 2019).

The question of unorthodoxy is more clearly inscribed in An-Na'im's engagement with the methods of the Islamic tradition through both dismissal and rejection. On the important question of sources, An-Na'im contends: '[t]he

---

[44] If we compare the teachings of the Almohad founder Ibn Tumart and Ibn Rushd, they share a unanimity of ideas, save for their views on the aspect of the Almohad founders' support and endorsement of the Ash'arites. Ibn Rushd consistently disagreed with the tradition of Ash'ari kalam, on the basis that it espoused dialectical arguments which produced imprecise and unreliable interpretations. Urvoy suggests that Ibn Rushd might have been responsible for the change in the official Almohad stance towards the work of al-Ghazali, through his sustained theological attacks on the methods of *kalam* (Urvoy 1991, pp. 72–80).

[45] After all, orthodoxy in Islamic intellectual history also constituted the debates and informal opinions of scholars which gained 'public recognition' (Jackson, 2002, p. 30).

The Pluralistic Frameworks 61

Islamic argument for a secular state that I am making is in terms of a paradigm or framework for thinking about the issues, and not a hermeneutical or exegetical analysis of Islamic sources which needs to be based on an agreed interpretative framework to be persuasive' (An-Na'im, 2008, p. xi). An-Na'im's rationale for this position is that a hermeneutical argument that lacks an agreed interpretative framework can simply be countered by an opposing interpretation based on another framework. But the veritable void of such an argument which seeks to develop a substantive theory for human rights and constitutionalism in Islam is exactly its dismissal of existing methods. The question of paucity of sources extend to An-Na'im's engagement with the Islamic theological schools and with the ethical debates within the Islamic moral tradition. In a cursory reference, An-Na'im acknowledges Islamic speculative theology (*kalām*) as one of the aspects of *sharī'a* developed by 'independent scholars' during the formative centuries of Islam (An-Na'im, 2008, p. 285). This brief listing of *kalām* alongside the science of jurisprudence (*fiqh*) is a point of historical context rather than a substantive engagement of its role in Islamic tradition. Although An-Na'im refers to al-Ghazali as one of the 'most authoritative Sunni scholars of all time', he is not invested in amplifying the existence or centrality of traditional authority in the Islamic tradition, choosing instead to selectively criticise such ideas in line with his argument for a secular state (An-Na'im, 2008, pp. 10, 50). His noted 'disappointment' with Islamic modernist thinkers such as Al-Afghani and Rida as well as his inclination for promoting the ideas of Islamic thinkers like Ibn Rushd, Ali ibn Raziq, and Fazlur Rehman suggest that this selective criticism is tactical: to liberalise and reform *sharī'a* (An-Na'im, 1990, pp. 61, 67).

One may infer from this lack of elaboration that An-Na'im also appears to be distancing himself from the traditional emphasis placed on theological debates and their implications for political frameworks within Islam. This is a plausible claim given An-Na'im's project of separating Islamic thought from its traditional theological underpinnings in order to advance a rationalistic and liberal conception of Islamic law and ethics which negotiates *sharī'a* to achieve a reconciliation with liberal ideals such as human rights and democracy. In other words, by dismissing traditional Islamic methods anchored in theological debates, An-Na'im can circumvent important normative and textual questions as they relate to foundational questions of creed and reinterpret *sharī'a* through a primarily liberal lens more easily. For An-Na'im, Muslims can authentically embrace liberal values from within an Islamic framework, without having to conform to predetermined notions of what qualifies as being 'sufficiently Muslim whether in Western or conservative Islamic discourse' (An-Na'im, 2008, p. 269). Ostensibly, the unorthodoxy of this approach does not only lie in its dismissal of the methods of the Islamic tradition, but in its call for redefining the terms for Islamic authenticity.

As a legal scholar, An-Na'im's engagement with the methods of Islamic jurisprudence is more rigorous and substantive. Presumably this is because of the centrality of *sharī'a* as a jurisprudential tradition for Muslims: 'I am calling for mediation rather than confrontation in this regard, because I know that if I, as a Muslim, am faced with a stark choice between Islam and human rights, I will certainly opt for Islam' (An-Na'im, 2008, p. 111). He dedicates a chapter of his book on Islamic legal reform to elaborate on the Islamic jurisprudential tradition pointing to some of the 'controversies' surrounding its development, such as the authenticity of sources and the problems with the evolution of legal norms (An-Na'im, 1996, pp. 16–17). He outlines the sources and techniques employed by jurists in establishing a consensus of four schools of jurisprudential thought as the basis of Islamic legal normativity. One of his main points of critique surrounds the principle of *taqlid*, the close and faithful following by contemporary Muslims to one of these jurisprudential schools as opposed to resorting directly to their own reasoned interpretations (An-Na'im, 1996, p. 18). Islamic legal reform, for An-Na'im, requires abandoning these intermediaries as they offered limited scope for transforming the rules and principles of the public law of *sharī'a* (An-Na'im, 1996, p. 19). Islam's foundational text, the Qur'an, he maintains, is regarded as complete and beyond dispute by Muslims: 'what needs to be re-examined ... is the use of the Qur'an as the basis of positive law' (An-Na'im, 1996, p. 19). Taha offers Muslims a way out, as it were, by formulating a methodology that can promote a 'humane and enlightened message of Islam', consistent with the precepts of 'human dignity and freedom' (An-Na'im, 1990, p. 54). March quite correctly identifies An-Na'im's method as an instance of holding a 'religious nomocracy', like Islam, 'to an ontological standard to which few orthodox Muslims have aspired' (March, 2015, p. 113). Unsurprisingly, a common refrain of An-Na'im's scholarship is the dialectic between heresy and orthodoxy:

> [S]ince every orthodoxy started as a heresy, we must protect, indeed celebrate, the possibility of heresy in order to ensure the relevance and future development of *sharī'a*. For every heresy we suppress, we miss the possibility of an idea or principle that future generations of Muslims may wish to establish as part of their orthodox Islam. I say that no human being should have that power to control what others may wish to believe or disbelieve. (An-Na'im, 2008, p. 293)

For An-Na'im, defying orthodoxy is crucial for the internal transformation of Islam while the protection of dissent and heresy is essential for the authenticity and vitality of Islamic discourse. Both can be harnessed through the 'power of

The Pluralistic Frameworks 63

ideas' expounded 'in the right way at the right time' to achieve progress (An-Na'im, 1990, p. 186). Through this recognition, An-Na'im's conception of *sharī'a*, I suggest, can be thought of as valorising the concept of heresy insofar as it achieves its objectives of inspiring social and political change. Although An-Na'im argues that Muslims need not necessarily accept Taha's specific arguments in support of the secular state, his embrace of Taha's foundational approach – which constitutes a radical and provocative departure from Islamic orthodoxy – comes at a cost, which he appears to accept:

> [T]o face the question of practical acceptability ... it may appear that the prospect of wide acceptance and implementation of Ustadh Mahmoud's evolutionary principle by the majority of Muslims in the near future does not seem to be promising. This is not only because the principle itself presents such a drastic break with the long tradition of Islamic jurisprudence but also because it raises the prospect of serious challenge to the vested interest of powerful forces in the Muslim world. (An-Na'im, 1990, p. 67)

Reimagining *sharī'a* as public law is not without merit and continues to shape Islamic reformist approaches in the contemporary context. Such debates consider why *sharī'a* norms such as holy war (*jihād*), apostasy laws, and rules for non-Muslims within a state (*dhimma*) must be enacted or set aside. Such debates remain unsettled and contested and are often nominally adopted by Muslim-majority societies. An-Na'im's own analysis reflects a complexity of existing systems in Muslim-majority societies where *sharī'a* plays a highly variegated, localised, and fluctuating role in shaping laws that govern Muslim public life. Indonesia, the most populous Muslim country in the world, is an interesting case study that An-Na'im refers to. The Indonesian model of pluralism, as An-Na'im points out, suggests there is a range of views on the relationship between Islam and the state, rather than just the extreme positions of complete fusion or total separation (An-Na'im, 2008, p. 266). At its democratic inception Indonesia constructed a form of 'covenantal pluralism' which allowed religion to remain at the centre of public life with some *sharī'a* norms being enacted in local contexts but without serving as a legislative foundation for the state. As Hefner notes:

> Indonesia seemed to have put in place many of the ingredients required to create a civic pluralism of a broadly covenantal sort [including] [i]n matters of legislation, Islamic education, and the all-important question of intellectual leadership and mass-organisational support for democracy and plural citizenship. (Hefner, 2020, p. 8)

The Indonesian case study, while not theorised in political terms, I suggest, is useful for thinking about normative possibilities for Islamic politics in the future. The discursive site for such possibilities is a better theorisation of concepts such as tolerance, pluralism, and citizenship in Islam and as it relates to its existing ethico-legal tradition.[46] While some scholars are undertaking this crucial endeavour, more work is required in this regard.

The second important insight that we may gain from examining the pluralistic frameworks of these thinkers concerns the notion of *Islamic tradition* and the secularist impulse to call for its reformation – that is, to argue for its inherent lack of ability to develop a language that coheres with liberalism. Within this secular purview, Islamic tradition is staged as being in an unresolvable confrontation with modernity. This sentiment is captured in the following statement by Roy: '[S]ince the time of the original community there has always been a de facto autonomous political space in the Muslim world: what has been lacking is a political thought regarding the autonomy of this space, which has therefore been perceived by the traditionalists as contingent and by the Islamists as deviant' (Roy, 1994, p. 14). Such critiques of the Islamic tradition suggest that there is something intrinsic to the 'Islamic political imagination', which cannot move beyond the idea of a political ethics derived from law. Islam's animating impulse is to legitimate politics through law, something Makdisi describes as its 'nomocratic and nomocentric' characteristics (Makdisi, 1981, p. 264). Evidently there are important questions here for scholars of Islamic intellectual history:

> The intellectual historian of Islam must ask how, to what extent, and why Islamic tradition became 'nomocratic and nomocentric'; in what ways were law and politics related; to what extent it is legitimate to represent traditional bodies of *fiqh* through modern concepts of law and medieval Islamic views on governance through modern political theories; and what is gained and lost in such representation. (Anjum, 2012, p. 22)

Anjum's key point about Islamic tradition being defined through nomocracy is useful when evaluating the pluralistic frameworks of these thinkers. It calls for a reflexive engagement with the Islamic intellectual tradition that does not obscure or oversimplify the historical link between law and politics in Islam. It beckons at a greater nuance on understanding the myriad manifestations of Islamic governance as conceptualised in the Islamic tradition, including the forms in which juridico-religious authority and political authority remained

---

[46] Recent jurisprudential debates suggest that innovative reasoning is being applied to provide a new Islamic discourse on tolerance and citizenship which affirms the importance of political pluralism. Scholars such as Auda (2008) and Abou El Fadl (2017) have advanced sophisticated reinterpretations of *sharī'a* by applying the juristic principle of purposes of the law (*maqasid-as-sharī'a*) to argue in favour of Islamic pluralist models that promote a broader ethics of human welfare. Moreover, when it comes to public laws in Muslim-majority countries, there is also significant diversity in how select *sharī'a* principles are incorporated and interpreted, with some countries like Malaysia and Morocco opting for mixed legal systems.

independent and remained intertwined. After all, in the Islamic tradition there existed 'veritable tendencies that theorised a positive role for political life and action and saw law as only one of Islam's many complementary manifestations' (Anjum, 2012, p. 26). Some may argue that the notion of a nomocratic Islamic tradition poses significant challenges for the development of modern Islamic political thought or for future pluralistic frameworks. Such a critique, I suggest risks foisting onto the Islamic tradition a set of a priori assumptions about law and politics, a larger methodological problem identified in the literature of comparative political theory. As this Element reveals, Islam as a discursive tradition continues to evolve and incorporate new conceptual frames and political categories over time through pluralistic engagement, synthesisation and dialogue. Preserving Islamic tradition should not preclude the possibility of theoretical re-imagination. Future studies should also aim to identify, foreground, and analyse the contours of other pluralistic frameworks in the *longue durée* of Islamic intellectual history.

Iqtidar (2016) offers us a valuable conceptual framing for understanding the Islamic tradition by introducing the notion of *method and sensibility*. Here, the Islamic tradition is conceptualised as a system of thought and practice that includes both a method and a sensibility which allow it to 'sustain debate, difference and questioning without being overcome and transformed completely by them' (Iqtidar, 2016, p. 431). In this proposed definition of tradition, method refers to the ways in which knowledge is produced and transmitted within a tradition, while sensibility refers to the philosophical and ethical outlook that informs that tradition. Iqtidar makes a powerful case for why two key elements of the Islamic jurisprudential tradition – to follow (*taqlīd*) and its relationship to independent and creative juridical interpretation (*ijtihād*) – are relevant to the discussion of method and sensibility and tell us something about the vibrancy and vitality of Islamic thought (Iqtidar, 2016, p. 425). While the former provides a foundation for tradition, the latter provides scope for innovative applications to address contemporary challenges. Both these concepts, nourished in a variety of scholarship on *sharī'a*, demonstrate that 'vehement debate, contradictions and internal contestation are not signs of decay but of vitality within a tradition' (Iqtidar, 2016, p. 424). The extent to which these methods can be leveraged to complement the task of Islamic political thinkers in developing creative normative proposals remains an open and critically important question for further scholarly inquiry and debate.[47]

The appreciation of method and sensibility in the Islamic tradition also provides a useful lens for evaluating pluralistic frameworks. A key argument

---

[47] Islamic ethical debates on bioethics, environmental sustainability, and economic justice instantiate how these methods are employed to address modern social and political challenges.

posited by this comparative inquiry is that Ibn Rushd and An-Na'im advance unconventional and theologically innovative methods that depart from the Islamic tradition. But this approach, I suggest, can be considered alongside other strategies which may align to the sensibilities of the Islamic tradition. After all, the objective of harmonising and reconciling *sharī'a* with extra-Islamic traditions of political thought is a complex task with many moving parts. This point is more usefully illustrated when examining Ibn Rushd's pluralistic framework rather than An-Na'im's. Consider, for example, Ibn Rushd's envisioned Islamic polity. While Platonic in form, it adopts *sharī'a* as the basis for political legitimacy. Religious obligations like prayer and fasting are construed as political rights/duties with moral-political ends (Rosenthal, 1953). *Sharī'a*'s role is teleologically framed – to foster happiness within the Islamic political community. Political authority is virtuous rule and the idea that *sharī'a* must be taught at the appropriate level is presented as a key task of the ruler. Is Ibn Rushd appealing here to an ethical sensibility of the Islamic tradition? Arguably so.

Contrastingly, in An-Na'im's political thought, we can observe an approach that undermines both *method and sensibility* by intuitively placing the Islamic tradition in 'flux' and emphasising its fluidity and uncertainty (Philpott, 2008).[48] Such an approach is underlined by his proposition of a radical methodology for the reform of *sharī'a* on the basis that it is the product of human interpretation and therefore open to constant reinterpretation and change. As Philpott argues, if An-Na'im asserts that everything, including *sharī'a* interpretation, is in constant flux, then his very argument from that premise of flux cannot itself be stated as an unchanging truth. This self-contradictory nature of an argument from flux undermines its validity as a basis for advocating a secular state in Islam. Stemming from this contradiction, An-Na'im's account could be construed by Muslim critics as tenuously upholding an 'Islamic framework' as a form of secularism in disguise. His aspiration to join parallel ranks in the Islamic tradition by advancing this Islamic framework may also be considered as cavalier, if not polemical. An 'Islamic justification' for a secular state that is not generated from flux might require an investigation of how liberal notions of the 'secular' or of 'human rights' are expressed in the language and vocabulary of the Islamic tradition and defended in different terms. What is ultimately required from An-Na'im is a more thoughtful interrogation of the political term 'secular' which reveals it as less of a benign construct and more as a doctrine with an internal logic of its own. For devout Muslims to be more receptive to

---

[48] See Daniel Philpott, "Arguing with An- Na'im," Immanent Frame, 14 July 2008, accessed 2 June 2023; find at http://blogs.ssrc.org/tif/2008/07/14/arguing-with-annaim.

pluralistic frameworks that attempt to reconcile liberal thought and Islam such a mediation effort cannot solely rely on procedural mechanisms, consensus-building, or pragmatic concerns for stability, as Philpott (2008) argues. Rather, it needs to be grounded in transcendent foundations that resonate with core Islamic metaphysical and moral tenets. This is especially true for An-Na'im's defense of the principle of 'civic reason' which is central to his argument for a secular state.

I shall conclude with a few remarks on the utility of pluralistic frameworks for the future of Islamic politics. It is evident that pluralistic frameworks offer a range of normative possibilities to rethink Islamic politics in creative and imaginative ways. However, the success of this normative rethinking is contingent on the plausibility of its approach to Islamic ethics. A convincing proposal for an Islamic audience will require engaging with the range of existing sources and internal debates within Islamic legal theory. Without this engagement, the possibility of generating new political ideas that are persuasive to Muslims who take the centrality and authority of *sharī'a* as key to their self-understanding is severely limited. A successful normative rethinking of Islamic politics will also require carefully assessing the link between Islamic ethics and politics so as to ensure that the latter never assumes a complete independence of purpose and instrumentality. It will also require giving thought to which, (if any), individual political ends can be viewed as distinct from ethical and moral considerations, especially as regards questions of public morality. It is likely that such considerations will continue to be debated and contested but broad principles of agreement can be developed for the future.

The kind of pluralistic engagement that Islamic scholars seek is also crucial for the success of this normative endeavour. Given the dominance of European and Anglo-American political thought, Muslim thinkers, by dint of exposure and training, are likely to engage with extra-Islamic traditions of thought that arise from these contexts. Yet inscribed into the modern part of this canon is the dominant liberal tradition with its conceptual reimagining of ethics and politics, which demarcates the political as a sovereign domain of motivation and purpose and sharply sequestrates it from social and ethical rationality. Islamic thinkers who aim to mediate Islamic ethics and politics by reconciling *sharī'a* and liberal political thought must therefore consider the origins and presuppositions of these ideas. Idris' (2021b) study on Rawls' treatment of the 'Muslim Question' in *The Law of Peoples* argues that Rawls' approach to understanding Islam and global politics is myopic. It tends (Idris argues) to deflect attention away from colonial violence and economic exploitation and towards the ideals and good intentions of liberal societies. The effect is to obscure the complex geopolitical realities that underlie global conflicts, and to reinforce a simplistic and essentialised view of

Islam (Idris, 2021b, p. 114). Idris' broader point suggests the need for a critical-historical approach in understanding the genealogy of philosophical devices. Islamic thinkers – whether they choose pluralistic engagement with liberal, communitarian, or socialist ideas – must employ a critical and reflective awareness and sensibility. It would be interesting, for example, to see what kind of normative possibilities emerge if Islamic thinkers develop pluralistic frameworks by incorporating ideas, texts, and thinkers from other intellectual traditions – for example, from African, Latin American, or Chinese thought.

The success of pluralistic frameworks will also depend on the rigour and sincerity of Islamic thinkers in interacting with endogenous modes of Islamic legal and theological sources to develop fresh and innovative political theories that reflect on contemporary political realities in the Islamic world. Concepts such as democratic citizenship or constitutionalism could be productively rethought through this interaction. An example may be instructive here. In recent political writings, the Tunisian Muslim Democrat Rached Ghannouchi (2022) breaks away from existing allegiances to Islamism and formulates a new conceptual language for accepting a form of politics defined through 'public reason' (March, 2023). Ghannouchi's public reason approach finds its primary expression in Islamic legal normativity through the principle of *maqāsid al-sharī'a*, which refers to the objectives or purposes of Islamic law. According to this principle, the objective of Islamic law is to promote the welfare and well-being of human beings, both individually and collectively, through five main priorities: life, religion, lineage, property, and intellect (Ghannouchi, 2022). Ghannouchi presents the objectives of this principle of *sharī'a* as consistent with forms of contemporary democratic governance, arguing that they both serve the common purpose of promoting the public good and protecting the rights and freedoms of all members of society. As March argues, Ghannouchi's public reason approach to Islamic politics develops a shared understanding of the common good that is based on reason and evidence rather than on religious or ideological dogma, but which calls for consistency with the values of Islam (March, 2023, p. 26). Ghannouchi's rethinking of Islamic politics is a recognition of Muslim social life as a plural and conflicting arena that cannot be resolved or theorised through consensus; it values non-violent democratic politics as a way to manage social differences, even without prior religious or moral consensus (Ghannouchi, 2022).

Notably, Ghannouchi draws from a wide-ranging plurality of perspectives internal to the Islamic tradition to make a normative case for Islamic democracy and human rights. This prioritisation 'of politics over theory and doctrine', March argues, represents an important historic turn for Islamic political thought (March, 2023, p. 26). It signals an evolution towards more pragmatic engagement with political ideas. Ghannouchi's method begins with the realities of modern plural societies and the democratic political process, and then works to harmonise these with Islamic principles and values. In a section on 'flexibility in applying Islamic principles to local governance', Ghannouchi remarks on the importance of pluralistic intellectual inquiry: 'It is good to recall the excellent words of our North African sage Abu al-Walid Ibn Rushd (d. 585 H/1198 CE) as he emphasised the necessity of benefiting from the best human experiments regardless of their religious origins, since wisdom is *sharīʿa*'s twin' (Ghannouchi, 2022, p. 20). Ibn Rushd's statement on the utility of methodological pluralism resonates with Ghannouchi's search to develop a political order consistent with Islamic principles and values while recognising the importance of democratic governance and political pluralism.

Hallaq offers two courses of action for a future Islamic politics. The first is for Muslims to develop governance models based on moral communities which transcend the sovereign state model (Hallaq, 2013, p. 169). The second is for Muslims to engage with extra-Islamic traditions of thought that challenge universalist theories of rights while restating the importance of morality. Both proposed courses depend on a 'discursive negotiation' between 'east and west' that is gradual and procedural, but that promotes mutual benefits for liberal and Islamic societies. For Hallaq, such benefits include strengthening global peace, intellectual enrichment, moral reform, the increased relevance of Islamic ethics, and the development of governance models that align with Islamic principles while engaging with the modern world (Hallaq, 2013, pp. 169–170). From the vantage point of Muslims, Hallaq proposes a promising outline for the future of Islamic ethics and politics. Yet how else might Islamic thinkers pursue the normative possibilities of reimagining Islamic politics in a rapidly changing world in which environmental and technological changes present new challenges for ethical consideration? Given the inadequacy of the modern sovereign state, what alternative political imaginaries are possible and what would they look like? What forms of political rethinking and arguments for political action are required for mitigating against such challenges and how can *sharīʿa* as a manifestation of Islamic ethics offer alternative approaches? These are difficult questions but need to be urgently theorised and addressed for reimagining a future Islamic politics. The task of Islamic thinkers is to consider *how* pluralistic frameworks can aid in securing this future.

Bibliography

Abou El Fadl, K. (2013). 'The sharī'a'. In J. Esposito & E. Shahin (eds.), *The Oxford Handbook of Islam and Politics* (pp. 7–26). Oxford: Oxford University Press.

Adamson, P. & Di Giovanni, M. (eds.). (2018). *Interpreting Averroes: Critical Essays*. Cambridge: Cambridge University Press.

Anjum, O. (2007). Islam as a discursive tradition: Talal Asad and his interlocutors. *Comparative Studies of South Asia, Africa and the Middle East*, 27(3), pp. 656–672.

Anjum, O. (2012). *Politics, Law, and Community in Islamic Thought: The Taymiyyan Moment*. Cambridge: Cambridge University Press.

An-Na'im, A. A. (1986). The Islamic law of apostasy and its modern applicability: A case from the Sudan. *Religion*, 16(3), 197–224.

An-Na'im, A. A. (1990). *Toward an Islamic Reformation: Civil Liberties, Human Rights, and International Law*. Syracuse, NY: Syracuse University Press.

An-Na'im, A. A. (ed.) (1992). *Human Rights in Cross-Cultural Perspectives: A Quest for Consensus*. Philadelphia: University of Pennsylvania Press.

An-Na'im, A. A. (1998). Shari'a and positive legislation: Is an Islamic state possible or viable? *Yearbook of Islamic and Middle Eastern Law*, 5(1), pp. 29–41.

An-Na'im, A. A. (2008). *Islam and the Secular State*. Cambridge, MA: Harvard University Press.

An-Na'im, A. A. (2014). Islamic politics and the neutral state: A friendly amendment to Rawls? In T. Bailey & V. Gentile (eds.), *Rawls and Religion* (pp. 242–265). New York: Columbia University Press.

Aristotle (1996). *The Politics and Constitution of Athens*, ed. S. Everson, trans. B. Jowett. Cambridge: Cambridge University Press.

Aristotle (2000). *Nicomachean Ethics*, trans. R. Crisp. Cambridge: Cambridge University Press.

Arkoun, M. (1994). Rethinking Islam today. *Annals of the American Academy of Political and Social Science*, 588(1), pp. 18–39.

Asad, T. (1993). *Genealogies of Religion: Discipline and Reasons of Power in Christianity and Islam*. Baltimore, MD: Johns Hopkins University Press.

Asad, T. (1999). Religion, nation-state, secularism. In P. van der Veer & L. Hartmut (eds.), *Nation and Religion: Perspectives on Europe and Asia* (pp. 178–196). Princeton, NJ: Princeton University Press.

Bibliography 71

Asad, T. (2003). *Formations of the Secular: Christianity, Islam, Modernity*. Stanford, CA: Stanford University Press.

Asad, T. (2009). The idea of an anthropology of Islam. *Qui parle, 17*(2), pp. 1–30.

Auda, J. (2008). *Maqasid Al-Shari'ah as Philosophy of Islamic Law*. London: International Institute of Islamic Thought.

Bauer, T. (2021). *A Culture of Ambiguity: An Alternative History of Islam*. New York: Columbia University Press.

Belo, C. (2022). Averroes on family and property in the Commentary on Plato's 'Republic'. In A. Orwin (ed.), *Plato's Republic in the Islamic Context: New Perspectives on Averroes's Commentary* (pp. 113–132). Rochester, NY: University of Rochester Press.

Berman, L. V. (1967). Excerpts from the lost Arabic original of Ibn Rushd's 'Middle Commentary on the Nicomachean Ethics'. *Oriens, 20*, pp. 31–59.

Bilgrami, A. (2012). Secularism: Its content and context. *Economic and Political Weekly, 47*(4), pp. 89–100.

Black, A. (2001). *The History of Islamic Political Thought: From the Prophet to the Present*. Edinburgh: Edinburgh University Press.

Bouhafa, F. (2019). Averroes' corrective philosophy of law. In P. Adamson & Matteo Di Giovanni (eds.), *Interpreting Averroes: Critical Essays* (pp. 64–80). Cambridge: Cambridge University Press.

Butterworth, C. (2004). Ethical and political philosophy. In P. Adamson & R. Taylor (eds.), *The Cambridge Companion to Arabic Philosophy*. Cambridge Companions to Philosophy (pp. 266–286). Cambridge: Cambridge University Press.

Connolly, W. E. (1999). *Why I Am Not a Secularist*. Minneapolis: University of Minnesota Press.

Dallmayr, F. (2004). Beyond monologue: For a comparative political theory. *Perspectives on Politics, 2*(2), pp. 249–257.

Devji, F. & Kazmi, Z. (eds.). (2017). *Islam after Liberalism*. Oxford: Oxford University Press.

Di Giovanni, M. (2018). Averroes, philosopher of Islam. In P. Adamson & Matteo Di Giovanni (eds.), *Interpreting Averroes: Critical Essays*. (pp. 9–26). Cambridge: Cambridge University Press.

Eickelman, D. & Piscatori, J. (1996). *Muslim Politics*. Princeton, NJ: Princeton University Press.

El Amine, L. (2016). Beyond East and West: Reorienting political theory through the prism of modernity. *Perspectives on Politics, 14*(1), pp. 102–120.

El Shamsy, A. (2013). *The Canonization of Islamic Law: A Social and Intellectual History*. Cambridge: Cambridge University Press.

Emon, A. M. (2010). *Islamic Natural Law Theories*. New York: Oxford University Press.

Euben, R. L. (1997). Comparative political theory: An Islamic fundamentalist critique of rationalism. *Journal of Politics*, *59*(1), pp. 28–55.

Euben, R. L. (1999). *Enemy in the Mirror: Islamic Fundamentalism and the Limits of Modern Rationalism: A Work of Comparative Political Theory*. Princeton, NJ: Princeton University Press.

Fadel, M. (2008). The true, the good and the reasonable: The theological and ethical roots of public reason in Islamic law. *Canadian Journal of Law & Jurisprudence*, *21*(1), pp. 5–69.

Fadl, K. A. (2014). *Reasoning with God: Reclaiming Shari'ah in the Modern Age*. London: Rowman & Littlefield.

Fadl, K. A. (2017). Qur'anic ethics and Islamic law. *Journal of Islamic Ethics*, *1* (1/2), pp. 7–28. https://doi.org/10.1163/24685542-12340002.

Fakhry, M. (1991). *Ethical Theories in Islam*. Leiden: Brill.

Fakhry, M. (2001). *Averroës: His Life, Works and Influence*. Oxford: Oneworld.

Gellner, E. (1991). Islam and Marxism: Some comparisons. *International Affairs*, *67*(1), pp. 1–6.

Ghannouchi, R. (2022). *Public Freedoms in the Islamic State*, trans. D. Johnston. New Haven, CT: Yale University Press.

Ghannouchi, R. & March, A. F. (2023). *On Muslim Democracy: Essays and Dialogues*. New York: Oxford University Press.

Gutas, D. (2002). The study of Arabic philosophy in the twentieth century: An essay on the historiography of Arabic philosophy. *British Journal of Middle Eastern Studies*, *29*(1), pp. 5–25.

Habermas, J. (1989). *The Structural Transformation of the Public Sphere*. Cambridge, MA: MIT Press.

Habermas, J. (1995). Reconciliation through the public use of reason: Remarks on John Rawls' political liberalism. *Journal of Philosophy*, *92*(3), pp. 109–131.

Habermas, J. (2006). Religion in the public sphere. *European Journal of Philosophy*, *14*, pp. 1–25.

Habermas, J. (2008). Notes on post-secular society. *New Perspectives Quarterly*, *25* (4), pp. 17–29.

Haidar, H. H. (2006). Rawls and religion: Between the decency and justice of reasonable religious regimes. *Politics and Ethics Review*, *2*(1), pp. 62–78.

Hallaq, W. B. (1984). Was the gate of ijtihad closed? *International Journal of Middle East Studies*, *16*(1), pp. 3–41.

Hallaq, W. B. (2002). The quest for origins or doctrine: Islamic legal studies as colonialist discourse. *UCLA Journal of Islamic and Near Eastern Law*, *2*(1), pp. 1–32.

Bibliography

Hallaq, W. B. (2011). Maqasid and the challenges of modernity. *Al-Jami'ah: Journal of Islamic Studies*, *49*(1), pp. 1–31.

Hallaq, W. B. (2013). *The Impossible State: Islam, Politics, and Modernity's Moral Predicament*. New York: Columbia University Press.

Harvey, R. (2023). Whose justice? When Maturidi meets MacIntyre. *Justice in Islam: New Ethical Perspectives*. London: International Institute of Islamic Thought.

Hashemi, N. (2009). *Islam, Secularism, and Liberal Democracy: Toward a Democratic Theory for Muslim Societies*. New York: Oxford University Press.

Hefner, R. W. (2020). Islam and covenantal pluralism in Indonesia: A critical juncture analysis. *Review of Faith & International Affairs*, *18*(2), pp. 1–17.

Hobbes, T. ([1651] 2008). *Leviathan* (Gaskin, J.C.A Ed.). Oxford: Oxford University Press.

Hoover, J. (2007). *Ibn Taymiyya's Theodicy of Perpetual Optimism*. Leiden: Brill.

Hourani, A. (1983). *Arabic Thought in the Liberal Age 1798–1939*. Cambridge: Cambridge University Press.

Hourani, G. H. (1961). Introduction and notes. In G. H. Hourani (ed.), *Averroës: On the Harmony of Religion and Philosophy* (pp. 1–43). London: Luzac.

Hourani, G. F. (1985). *Reason and Tradition in Islamic Ethics*. Cambridge: Cambridge University Press.

Howard, W. S. (2001). Mahmoud Mohammed Taha and the Republican Brotherhood: Transforming Islamic society. *Journal for Islamic Studies*, *21*, pp. 71–84.

Huntington, S. P. (1993). The clash of civilizations? *Foreign Affairs*, *72*(3), pp. 22–28.

Ibn Rushd. (1954). *The Incoherence of the Incoherence*, trans. S. van den Bergh. Oxford: Oxford University Press.

Ibn Rushd. (1961). *On the Harmony of Religion and Philosophy*, trans. G. H. Hourani. London: Luzac.

Ibn Rushd. (1974). *Averroes Commentary on Plato's Republic*, trans. R. Lerner. Ithaca, NY: Cornell University Press.

Ibn Rushd. (2000). *The Distinguished Jurist's Primer* (2 vols.), trans. Imran Ahsan Khan Nyazee. Reading: Garnet.

Ibn Rushd (2001). *Exposition on Religious Arguments*, trans. E. Najjar. Oxford: Oneworld.

Idris, M. (2018). *War for Peace: Genealogies of a Violent Ideal in Western and Islamic Thought*. New York: Oxford University Press.

Idris, M. (2021a). Islam, Rawls, and the disciplinary limits of late twentieth-century liberal philosophy. *Modern Intellectual History*, *18*(4), pp. 1034–1057.

Idris, M. (2021b). The Kazanistan Papers: Reading the Muslim Question in the John Rawls Archives. *Perspectives on Politics*, *19*(1), pp. 110–130.

Iqtidar, H. (2011). *Secularizing Islamists? Jama'at-e-Islami and Jama'at-ud-Da'wa in Urban Pakistan*. Chicago, IL: University of Chicago Press.

Iqtidar, H. (2016). Redefining 'tradition' in political thought. *European Journal of Political Theory*, *15*(4), pp. 424–444.

Iqtidar, H. (2017). Introduction: Tolerance in modern Islamic thought. *ReOrient*, *2*(1), pp. 5–11.

Iqtidar, H. (2020). Theorizing popular sovereignty in the colony: Abul A'la Maududi's 'Theodemocracy'. *Review of Politics*, *82*(4), pp. 595–617.

Iqtidar, H. (2021). *Jizya* against nationalism: Abul a'la Maududi's attempt at decolonizing political theory. *Journal of Politics*, *83*(3), pp. 1145–1157.

Iqtidar, H. & Scharbordt, O. (2022). Divine sovereignty, morality and the state: Maududi and his influence. *Journal of the Royal Asiatic Society*, *32*(2), pp. 277–293.

Jackson, S. A. (2002). *On the Boundaries of Theological Tolerance in Islam: Abmid Al-Ghazâlî's Fay al Al-Tafriqa Bayna Al-Islâm Wa Al-Zandaqa*. Oxford: Oxford University Press.

Jenco, L. K. (2011). Recentering political theory: The promise of mobile locality. *Cultural Critique*, *79*, pp. 27–59.

Jenco, L. K., Idris, M., & Thomas, M. C. (2020). Introduction. In *Comparison, Connectivity, and Disconnection* (pp. 1–40). New York: Oxford University Press.

Kaminski, J. J. (2017). *The Contemporary Islamic Governed State: A Reconceptualization*. Cham: Palgrave MacMillan.

Kant, I. (1998). *Groundwork of the Metaphysics of Morals*, trans. M. Gregor. Cambridge: Cambridge University Press.

Kant, I. ([1785] 2012). *Kant: Groundwork of the Metaphysics of Morals*. Cambridge: Cambridge University Press.

Khan, S. (2017). Fallacies of foundational principles: Rawls's political liberalism and Islamophobia. *ReOrient*, *3*(1), pp. 50–64.

Kymlicka, W. (1995). *Multicultural Citizenship: A Liberal Theory of Minority Rights*. Oxford: Oxford University Press.

Leaman, O. (1980). Ibn Rushd on happiness and philosophy. *Studia Islamica*, *52*(1), pp. 167–181.

Leaman, O. (1988). *Averroës and His Philosophy*. Surrey: Curzon.

Leaman, O. (2014). *Controversies in Contemporary Islam*. New York: Routledge.

Lerner, R. (1974). Introduction and notes. In R. Lerner (ed.), *Averroës on Plato's Republic* (pp. xiii–xxviii). Ithaca, NY: Cornell University Press.

Lewis, B. (2002). *What Went Wrong? The Clash between Islam and Modernity in the Middle East*. New York: Oxford University Press.

Locke, J. ([1689] 1980). *Second Treatise of Eovernment*, ed. C. B. Macpherson. Cambridge: Hackett.

MacIntyre, A. ([1981] 2007). *After Virtue*. London: Bloomsbury Academic.

MacIntyre, A. (1988). *Whose Justice? Which Rationality?* Notre Dame, IN: Notre Dame University Press.

Makdisi, G. (1991). *Religion, Law and Learning in Classical Islam*. New York: Routledge.

March A. F. (2008). Islamic Legal Theory, Secularism and Religious Pluralism: Is Modern Religious Freedom Sufficient for the *Shari'a* 'Purpose [*Maqsid*]' of 'Preserving Religion [*Hifz Al-Din*]?' Islamic Law and Law of the Muslim World Paper No. 09–78, Yale Law School, Public Law Working Paper No. 208.

March, A. F. (2009). What is comparative political theory? *Review of Politics*, *71*(4), pp. 531–565.

March, A. F. (2011). *Islam and Liberal Citizenship: The Search for an Overlapping Consensus*. Oxford: Oxford University Press.

March, A. F. (2012). Islamic political thought. In G. Gaus, F. D'Agostino, & R. Muldoon (eds.), *The Routledge Companion to Social and Political Philosophy* (pp. 204–214). New York: Routledge.

March, A. F. (2015). Political Islam: Theory. *Annual Review of Political Science*, *18*(1), pp. 103–123.

March, A. F. (2019). *The Caliphate of Man: Popular Sovereignty in Modern Islamic Thought*. Cambridge, MA: Harvard University Press.

March, A. F. (2023). After sovereignty: From a hegemonic to agonistic Islamic political thought. *Political Theory*, 52(*2*), pp. 259–288.

Marenbon, J. (2007). Latin Averroism. In A. Akasoy, J. E. Montgomery, & P. E. Pormann (eds.), *Islamic Crosspollinations: Interactions in the Medieval Middle East* (pp. 135–147). Exeter: Short Run Press.

Maududi, A. A. (1960). *The Islamic Law and Constitution*, ed. and trans. K. Ahmed. Lahore: Islamic Publications.

Nanji, A. (1991). Islamic ethics. In P. Singer (ed.), *A Companion to Ethics* (pp. 106–118). Princeton, NJ: Princeton University Press.

O'Sullivan, D. P. (2003). Punishing apostasy: The case of Islam and Shari'a law re-considered (Doctoral dissertation, Durham University).

Omar, A. (2019). Ibn Rushd's *The Decisive Treatise*: A text for political reform. *Medieval History Journal*, *22*(1), pp. 131–155.

Philpott, D. (2008). Arguing with An- Na'im. *Immanent Frame*. 14 July. Accessed 2 June 2023. http://blogs.ssrc.org/ tif/ 2008/07/14/ arguing-with-annaim.

Qutb, S. (1996). *Social Justice in Islam*, trans. W. E. Shepard. Leiden: Brill.

Qutb, S. (2006). *Milestones*, ed. A. B. al-Mehri. Birmingham: Maktabah.

Rahman, F. (1982). *Islam and Modernity: Transformation of an Intellectual Tradition*. Chicago, IL: University of Chicago Press.

Rawls, J. (1993a). The law of peoples. *Critical Inquiry*, *20*(1), pp. 36–68.

Rawls, J. (1993b). *Political Liberalism*. New York: Columbia University Press.

Rawls, J. (1997). The idea of public reason revisited. *University of Chicago Law Review*, *64*(3), pp. 765–807.

Razek, A. A. (2012). *Islam and the Foundations of Political Power*, trans. M. Loutfi. Edinburgh: Edinburgh University Press.

Rosenthal, E. I. J. (1953). The place of politics in the philosophy of Ibn Rushd. *Bulletin of the School of Oriental and African Studies*, *15*(2), pp. 246–278.

Rosenthal, E. I. J. (1956). Introduction and notes. In E. I. J. Rosenthal (ed.), *Averroës Commentary on Plato's Republic* (pp. 1–18). Cambridge: Cambridge University Press.

Roy, O. (1994). *The Failure of Political Islam*. Cambridge, MA: Harvard University Press.

Said, E. W. (1978). *Orientalism*. London: Penguin Books.

Schacht, J. (1964). *An Introduction to Islamic Law*. Oxford: Clarendon.

Soroush, A. (1998). The evolution and devolution of religious knowledge. In C. Kurzman (ed.), *Liberal Islam: A Sourcebook* (pp. 244–251). Oxford: Oxford University Press.

Stewart, D. J. (2015). Shari'a. In G. Bowering (ed.), *Islamic Political Thought: An Introduction* (pp. 219–237). Princeton, NJ: Princeton University Press.

Strauss, L. (1988). *Persecution and the Art of Writing*. Chicago, IL: Chicago University Press.

Taha, M. M. (1987). *The Second Message of Islam*. Syracuse, NY: Syracuse University Press.

Taliaferro, K. (2017). Ibn Rushd and natural law: Mediating human and divine law. *Journal of Islamic Studies*, *28*(1), pp. 1–27.

Tampio, N. (2014). Islamic political thought. In T. Gibbons (ed.), *The Encyclopaedia of Political Thought* (pp. 1–10). Oxford: Blackwell.

Urvoy, D. (1991). *Ibn Rushd (Averroes)*. London: Routledge.

Von Kügelgen, A., A Call for Rationalism: "Arab Averroists" in the Twentieth Century, *Alif: Journal of Comparative Poetics*, 16, 97–132.

Wilson, M. B. (2008). The failure of nomenclature: The concept of 'orthodoxy' in the study of Islam. *Comparative Islamic Studies*, *3*(2), p. 169.

Zaman, M. Q. (2012). *Modern Islamic Thought in a Radical Age*. Cambridge: Cambridge University Press.

Acknowledgements

I owe an enormous debt of gratitude to the many people and institutions involved in the journey of the completion of this Element. A special thank you to all my wonderful colleagues at the Department of Political Studies at the University of the Witwatersrand – Nicole Beardsworth, Julian Brown, Siphiwe Dube, Joel Quirk, Ahmed Veriava, Thokozani Chilenga-Butao, Thandeka Ndebele, and Daryl Glaser – for their friendship, collegiality, and support. A special thank you to Lawrence Hamilton, who facilitated through the SA-UK Bilateral Research Chair in Political Theory, a visiting fellowship at the Centre for Political Thought at the University of Cambridge which enabled me to complete this writing project. The list of those who have provided intellectual engagement and encouragement in the past year is far too long to recount here, but I wish to make special mention of Tim Karayianides, Oula Khadoum, Nick Tampio, Laurence Piper, Moshibudi Motimele, Loubna El-Amine, Andrew March, Anaheed Al-Hardan, Jonathan Earle, James Furner, Vineet Thackur, Keith Breckenridge, Catherine Burns, Vasileios Syros, and the late Stephen Louw. At SOAS, University of London, where I am currently undertaking a British Academy International Fellowship, I am particularly grateful to Manjeet Ramgotra, Stephen Chan, Rochana Bajpai, and Onur Ulas Ince for stimulating discussions and for their continuous support. In the course of completing this Element, I was graciously hosted at the Center for Law and Religion at Emory University, Atlanta, where Abdullahi Ahmed An-Na'im, Whittney Barth, Silas Allard, and Ira Bedzow offered their time, insights, and support. Thank you to Georgis Steiros and the Department of Philosophy at the National and Kapodistrian University of Athens for inviting me to present the final version of this Element. David Boucher, Ruksana Osman, Saleem Badat, Lawrence Hamilton, and Peter Vale have served as mentors and guides throughout my academic journey and to them I am ever so grateful. Thank you to the series editor Leigh Jenco and the anonymous peer reviewers at Cambridge University Press who provided meticulous and perceptive engagement with this Element. I wish to thank my family and friends for their support and words of encouragement. Finally, to Ismail, Maryam, Asma, and Tariq, thank you for your love, care, and patience.

About the Author

Ayesha Omar is a senior lecturer in political theory in the Department of Political Studies (Wits) and a British Academy International Fellow (2023) at the Department of Politics and International Studies (SOAS, University of London). Whilst at SOAS she will be undertaking a three-year research project on the Liberal Engagements of Black Intellectual History in South Africa. Ayesha's research will be used in the development of an extensive book project for Cambridge University Press. Ayesha has published various articles and book chapters in comparative political theory and intellectual history of South Africa. She is co-editor of the two-volume series the Cambridge History of African Political Thought, and the recently published volume *Decolonisation: Revolution and Evolution* with David Boucher (Wits University Press, 2023).

Cambridge Elements ≡

Comparative Political Theory

Leigh K. Jenco
London School of Economics

Leigh K. Jenco (PhD, Chicago) works across the disciplinary platforms of political theory, intellectual history, and East Asian studies. She is the author of *Changing Referents: Learning Across Space and Time in China and the West* (Oxford, 2015) and has published articles in the *American Political Science Review, Journal of Asian Studies, Modern China,* and *Political Theory*.

About the Series
Responding to urgent concerns as well as analyzing long-standing issues, the Comparative Political Theory Elements series invites engagements with texts and media from multiple languages, genres, and time periods. Elements in this series demonstrate the viability and meaning of historically-marginalized bodies of thought for audiences beyond their place of origin, while maintaining attention to the rich particularity of diverse global reflections on politics.

Cambridge Elements

Comparative Political Theory

Elements in the Series

Settlers in Indian Country
Charles W. A. Prior

Reimagining Radical Democracy in the Global South: Emerging Paradigms from Colombia and Türkiye
Kaan Ağartan and Camilo Tamayo Gomez

Maimonides and Jewish Theocracy: The Human Hand of Divine Rule
Charles H. T. Lesch

The Pluralistic Frameworks of Ibn Rushd and Abdullahi Ahmed An-Na'im
Ayesha Omar

A full series listing is available at: www.cambridge.org/ECPT